PRAISE FOR MAN, MYT[H]

"In a passionate and yet gentle and balanced way, this thoughtful book addresses many questions with which people today struggle and can help believers share their faith more effectively. It injects a healthy dose of common sense into popular debates too often dominated by intemperate rhetoric and historically irresponsible claims. This book makes the Christian faith more intelligible, offering a valuable defense for God's truth."

—DR. CRAIG S. KEENER
PROFESSOR OF NEW TESTAMENT, ASBURY THEOLOGICAL SEMINARY;
AND AUTHOR, NIV® BIBLE BACKGROUND COMMENTARY

"Dr. Rice Broocks has written a comprehensive but highly accessible book defending the key tenets of the Christian faith. Based on cutting-edge scholarship in documentary history and New Testament studies, he marshals persuasive arguments for the reliability of the New Testament documents, for the historicity of the resurrection, and for the divinity and Messianic credentials of Jesus of Nazareth. Broocks's concern for, and long experience speaking to, college-aged students comes through on every page in this conversational but rigorous work of practical apologetics. I highly recommended it."

—DR. STEPHEN C. MEYER
AUTHOR, *SIGNATURE IN THE CELL*; AND PRESENTER,
TRUEU APOLOGETIC SERIES

"In *Man, Myth, Messiah* Rice Broocks takes a massive amount of historical research on Jesus and makes it accessible, interesting, and relevant for today. This book will both strengthen the belief of Christians and challenge the unbelief of skeptics. As Broocks demonstrates, Jesus has had more influence on history than any living person. Isn't it worth wrestling with the question Jesus said matters most: "Who do you say I am?" *Man, Myth, Messiah* will take you on a journey to explore the historical evidence for the resurrection and the powerful implications that has for your life."

—SEAN MCDOWELL, PHD
BIOLA UNIVERSITY PROFESSOR, INTERNATIONALLY RECOGNIZED
SPEAKER, AND BESTSELLING AUTHOR, *THE FATE OF THE APOSTLES*

"I highly recommend this volume to you as a way to answer tough questions, ground the proclamation of the gospel message, and be prepared to share these truths with others, all from one text. Dr. Broocks is a capable guide to bring us safely to our destination. There is no greater message in life than that the gospel proclamation is true, that it answers our deepest needs and questions, along with the incredible benefit of eternal life to all who believe."

—GARY R. HABERMAS, PHD
DISTINGUISHED PROFESSOR AND CHAIR, DEPARTMENT OF
PHILOSOPHY AND THEOLOGY, LIBERTY UNIVERSITY

"Rice Broocks has done it again. In *God's Not Dead* he traced the evidence for God's existence with the heart of a pastor. In *Man, Myth, Messiah* Rice turns his attention to the person of Jesus as he examines the most important question of history. Few people understand the connection between evidence and evangelism as well as Rice Broocks, and this book, once again, reveals his heart as an evangelist and teacher. *Man, Myth, Messiah* is more than an apologetics book. It provides the evidence and challenges you to share the case with others."

—J. WARNER WALLACE
COLD CASE DETECTIVE AND AUTHOR, *GOD'S CRIME
SCENE* AND *COLD-CASE CHRISTIANITY*

MAN, MYTH, MESSIAH

MAN, MYTH, MESSIAH

ANSWERING HISTORY'S GREATEST QUESTION

RICE BROOCKS

W PUBLISHING GROUP

AN IMPRINT OF THOMAS NELSON

Published in Nashville, Tennessee, by W Publishing Group, an imprint of Thomas Nelson.

Thomas Nelson titles may be purchased in bulk for educational, business, fund-raising, or sales promotional use. For information, please e-mail SpecialMarkets@ThomasNelson.com.

Unless otherwise noted, Scripture quotations are taken from the Holy Bible, New International Version®, NIV®. © 1973, 1978, 1984, 2011 by Biblica, Inc.™ Used by permission of Zondervan. All rights reserved worldwide.

Scriptures marked ESV are taken from the ESV® Bible (The Holy Bible, English Standard Version®), © 2001 by Crossway, a publishing ministry of Good News Publishers. Used by permission. All rights reserved.

Scriptures marked NASB are taken from New American Standard Bible®, © 1960, 1962, 1963, 1968, 1971, 1972, 1973, 1975, 1977, 1995 by The Lockman Foundation. Used by permission.

Scriptures marked NKJV are taken from the New King James Version®. © 1982 by Thomas Nelson. Used by permission. All rights reserved.

Scripture marked KJV is taken from the King James Version. Public domain.

Library of Congress Control Number: 2015951788

ISBN 978-0-8499-4856-5

Printed in the United States of America

16 17 18 19 20 RRD 6 5

To the Undecided

CONTENTS

CONTENTS

FOREWORD

FROM POPULAR CULTURE TO NEW TESTAMENT CIRCLES in particular, the topic of the historical Jesus is arguably the most prominent subject at the present time. It has been that way for at least two or three decades as well. Since at least the 1980s, scholars have been engaged in what has been dubbed as the "Third Quest for the Historical Jesus," beginning with the initial German movement back in the nineteenth century.

Into this contemporary milieu steps Dr. Rice Broocks, having penned his volume, *Man, Myth, Messiah: Answering History's Greatest Question*. It acquaints readers with a popular overview of some key questions and issues from the current interest in linking Jesus Christ to history. Yet this text doesn't spare or shy away from sharing some of the scholarly ideas and key quotations that frame the present discussions.

In order to achieve this sort of task, Dr. Broocks endeavors to start with basic principles, moving up to more involved issues. In the process, many of the chief questions, topics, and state-of-the-art approaches are introduced and addressed.

All of this combines to make this volume a valuable guide to contemporary studies. It is also a manual of additional data that can assist with addressing the big questions that consistently gather around this subject.

As the author of this work, Dr. Broocks brings a unique combination of traits to this project. He is a pastor of a thriving multi-ethnic congregation in the Nashville Tennessee area, with a worldwide ministry beyond that, reaching out primarily to university students; with many other books, as well as a research doctorate from Fuller Seminary, to his credit. But having said that, Rice has an insatiable drive to help build God's kingdom. Evangelism is his heartbeat. Unlike many in his profession, he realizes that such can only be built on a foundation of knowledge. Thus, there is no substitute for established truth that exudes into purposeful action. A dearth in either area can be disastrous for Christian ministry. That's why this is the second time that one of his books has been the basis for a full-length movie!

For reasons such as these, Dr. Broocks builds a Christian foundation from which we can then launch out into action in the world. That is obvious when, in the first three chapters, he introduces the topics of history, the "Minimal Facts Method," and the reliability of Scripture. The next three chapters present some of the historical basis for Jesus' crucifixion and resurrection, along with His uniqueness. The two subjects after that are devoted to Jesus' deity and the reality of the supernatural world.

Only after laying this foundation does he move to the believer's need to engage in both discipleship and evangelism. As mentioned, good foundations provide the launching grounds for moving into sound practical action. But then it was the same way in the New Testament too.

For just one or two examples among the many that could be cited here, Paul stated that when he preached to the Corinthians, he first presented the gospel message. When the factual side of the gospel was defined in the New Testament, the deity of Christ, along with his death and resurrection, was named. Then after laying out this foundation, the apostle encouraged a commitment to Jesus Christ (1 Corinthians 15:1–2). Likewise, when Peter preached his first Pentecost sermon, which started the church, he also laid out the historical gospel foundation before he led into the practical message of evangelism (Acts 2:22–41).

This is the approach taken in this book, as Dr. Broocks also develops the groundwork before explaining God's remedy. He is a qualified leader in these areas, and he has a heart for doing so as well. In chapter 2, for instance, he shows how the minimal historical foundation of Christianity is so strong that skeptical scholars even accept its bedrock truths. Since this is the case, why wouldn't someone take the next step and believe?

For reasons such as these, I highly recommend this volume to you as a way to answer tough questions, ground the proclamation of the gospel message, and be prepared to share these truths with others, all from one text. Dr. Broocks is a capable guide to bring us safely to our destination. There is no greater message in life than that the gospel proclamation is true, that it answers our deepest needs and questions, along with the incredible benefit of eternal life to all who believe.

—GARY R. HABERMAS, PhD
DISTINGUISHED PROFESSOR AND CHAIR, DEPARTMENT
OF PHILOSOPHY AND THEOLOGY, LIBERTY UNIVERSITY

INTRODUCTION
IT IS A THING MOST WONDERFUL

I BROKE THE UNWRITTEN CODE RECENTLY AND PICKED up a magazine while standing in the checkout line of the grocery store. I couldn't resist seeing what *Newsweek* had to say about Jesus Christ in its feature titled "The 100 People Who Shaped Our World." I should have known that it wouldn't be good. It was predictably written from a skeptical perspective with little pretense to try to hide the bias. It seems you are expected to be respectful in what you say about any other religion or revered religious figure—except Jesus Christ. Mysteriously, people feel the liberty to malign, disfigure, and reimagine Him as they choose. In this rather brief attempt at a summation of His life and impact, the article communicated the typical notion that we are really unable to know much about Jesus historically.

The impact of Jesus of Nazareth, the itinerant preacher whose teachings became the basis of one of the world's most practiced religions, is irrefutable. But the nature of the man has been debated time and time again as we view him through the lenses of scholars moving ever further away from the time period in which Jesus lived.

What was fairly shocking was the referral at the end of the article to a book by sociologist Reza Aslan for those who wanted to learn more about Jesus. Of all the authors and books by Christian theologians *Newsweek* could have referenced, it pointed the reader to a Muslim who doesn't believe the Gospels are reliable and denies Jesus being the Son of God. I'm not saying a Muslim can't write about Jesus Christ; it's just that, at least, someone who could give a Christian perspective should have been referenced. So much for fair and balanced journalism.

This seems par for the course when it comes to the majority of portrayals of Jesus Christ in the secular media. Consistent historical methodology is kicked to the curb in favor of pushing the narrative of skepticism. What is also on display is the strange tendency, when it comes to writing about Jesus, to be disqualified from being referenced as a credible spokesperson if you call yourself a Christian. I can't think of any other area or issue where this would not be seen as unreasonable. That's like saying if you're an American you can't be trusted to talk authoritatively about the true facts of American history.

This type of consistently slanted presentation has contributed to the dramatic shift in the religious beliefs of those in the United States—especially those under thirty. This phenomenon has been labeled "the rise of the nones," specifically those that claim no religious affiliation. Pew Research Center states, "As a rising cohort of highly unaffiliated Millennials reaches adulthood, the median age of unaffiliated adults has dropped to 36, down from 38 in 2007 and far lower than the general (adult) population's median age of 46."[1]

Though the numbers are not as grim as some would have us believe, this trend is not something to ignore. There has definitely been an erosion of confidence in the credibility of the Christian faith—particularly among young people. At the heart of this crisis is one question that must be answered clearly in order to stop this downward pattern: Is the Christian story true?

Motivated by this alarming statistical data, I wrote the book *God's Not Dead: Evidence for God in an Age of Uncertainty*. The book would inspire a movie by the same name, and millions who watched it would know what it means to become defenders of the faith—specifically that God exists. Both the book and the movie sought to clearly establish the fact that real faith isn't blind. It is based on evidence. *God's Not Dead*, the book, laid out that evidence from science, philosophy, history, and Scripture.

Now in the sequel, *Man, Myth, Messiah*, we take a closer look at the evidence for the historical Jesus. The central contention that is set forth is that the Jesus of history is the Christ of faith. The Christian faith goes beyond simply declaring God exists and claims that God became man in Jesus Christ, lived among us, and ultimately sacrificed His life in order to atone for our sins. Three days after His death, He would rise again, proving that He was the Son of God, the promised Messiah, and the Savior of the world.

Christianity is the only religion that places the entire weight of its credibility on a singular event, the resurrection, which is a supernatural miracle. The following chapters demonstrate that the evidence from history, which even skeptics would accept, establishes that the resurrection is both the clear and best explanation for the widely accepted facts: Jesus' execution at the hands of Pontius Pilate, the discovery of His empty tomb by His women followers, the claims by His disciples that they had seen Him alive after His crucifixion, and many other events. If Christ had not been raised, then Christianity would be completely discredited and unworthy of even a moment's consideration, or as the apostle Paul stated, "And if Christ has not been raised, your faith is futile" (1 Corinthians 15:17).

Conviction about the reality of the resurrection is the only foundation that can withstand the onslaught of skepticism and unbelief. It is this fact that points to other critical truths, such as the authority of Scripture and the unique role of Jesus as Messiah and Savior. *Man, Myth, Messiah* provides key insights as to why the crucifixion and resurrection point to the fact that Jesus Christ is indeed the promised Messiah. The challenges from pop culture that the Jesus story is merely a myth or legend are shown to be the *real* myth. These types of speculative theories abound in a culture attempting to jump to warp speed in its flight away from God.

What is helping restrain that suicidal leap has been a renaissance in Christian apologetics and philosophy. Churches are starting to realize that equipping people to defend their faith is just as vital as teaching the basic doctrines, or preaching comforting and encouraging messages on Sunday.

I think it would be safe to say that no one's life or death in the history of the world has been studied, analyzed, debated, and heralded to the world as much as Jesus Christ of Nazareth. It's definitely a daunting task to respond to all of the theories and claims made by critics. During the process of research and writing, I felt the great sense of drama and significance of what is at stake in a study of whether the story is really true or, as skeptics assert, merely a collection of tales attempting to communicate the faith of the early Christians. Millions of people are apparently in the process of reassessing their beliefs. If that's true, they need to make decisions on the basis of credible evidence, not rumor or hearsay.

Regardless of who you are or where you were born, eventually you must make a decision about what you believe about this Man and the claim that He is the Son of God, the Savior of the world. Because of the gravity of the subject matter, I tried avoiding the everyday analogies and metaphors that are a part of my natural communication style, fearing my efforts would trivialize any number of the important aspects of the story. However, this thought process was eventually abandoned. For the most part, it was because of the realization that every follower of Christ must convey his faith through his own language and personalities. Whether written or spoken, we tell others the story of why we believe and the effect faith has had on our lives and the world around us. This is what has happened for two thousand years, starting with the testimonies of Matthew, Mark, Luke, and John, the men who wrote down the first biographies about the life of Jesus, and then continued by others for more than fifty generations.

Answering the Great Question

The collective task of proclaiming this message has been called the *Great Commission*, a term coined by Christian theologians and missiologists to describe the charge that Jesus gave His disciples to go into all the world and make disciples (Matthew 28:19–20). The *Great Commandment* is the term for the premier commandment Jesus gave us to love one another (John 13:35). So perhaps it would be fitting to describe what Jesus asked His disciples, "Who do you say that I am?" (Matthew 16:15 NKJV) as the *Great Question*—without a doubt, history's *greatest* question. The answer to this affects everything. And if we focus so heavily on the Great Commission and the Great Commandment, shouldn't we be giving equal attention to the Great Question?

In the Scriptures, the moment of that important question came quite abruptly, like a dreaded pop quiz in a classroom setting. It was asked after a series of dramatic, mind-blowing events: Jesus healing the blind and the lame, miraculously feeding five thousand people from five loaves of bread and two fish (then walking on water), and subsequently feeding another multitude of four thousand people from seven loaves of bread and a few fish.

These miracles were called "signs" in John's gospel. A sign points to something. If you see an Exit sign, you intuitively know it's pointing to a door that you can walk through. These signs pointed to the fact that Jesus was no ordinary man. He was the promised one, the Son of God. Jesus then asked the Great Question, "Who do you say I am?" The lone voice that immediately answered was the outspoken disciple Peter. He said, "You are the Messiah, the Son of the living God" (Matthew 16:15–16). If this declaration had not been true, Jesus would have instantly corrected such a brash and blasphemous claim. No true prophet of God would have allowed such a pernicious misunderstanding to persist.

Jesus didn't correct or rebuke Peter for his stunning revelation but instead praised him by saying, "Blessed are you, Simon son of Jonah, for this was not revealed to you by flesh and blood, but by my Father in heaven." He went on to tell him that He would build His church on this very foundation—one that "the gates of Hades will not overcome" (Matthew 16:17–18). In this exchange between Peter and the Lord, we see the battle line drawn in the sand. And this battle would cost many of Jesus' followers their very lives.

The cosmic struggle would come down to the knowledge of the true identity of this man from Nazareth in the northern region of Galilee in the tiny nation of Israel. The promise was made that regardless of the fierceness of the conflict, the powers of darkness would not prevail. In light of this exchange, it becomes clear why there has been such a firestorm around the name of Jesus Christ. No other name evokes such debate or emotion—the most popular as well as the most polarizing name in history. At the same time, no other name has inspired such beauty, courage, and sacrifice.

The Voice

One of the most popular shows on American television is *The Voice*. It is yet another talent show inspired by *Britain's Got Talent* and *American Idol*. For those who haven't seen it, the judges turn their backs on the contestants and hear them sing without getting to see them visibly. Each judge picks the voice he likes the most and then turns his chair around to see who it is he has chosen. This might be one of the best examples of how we decide what voice we will listen to and follow when it comes to spiritual truths.

Well into the twenty-first century, it now feels as though the entire set of rules in Western civilization is being overturned, much like the upheaval at the start of the twentieth century that surrounded the laws of science and nature (relativity and the quantum theory).

Every moral and social structure seems to now be up for grabs—to be redefined in the name of tolerance and freedom. The only voices of opposition to this social and moral revolution are those that appear to be religiously motivated. Some of those voices are reactionary, fearful, and intolerant. However, there is another voice that doesn't scream or shout but has faithfully spoken from age to age regarding the nature of God and humanity. This is the loving voice of our Creator—not a distant, impersonal force, or detached first cause, but a loving merciful God. This God was powerful enough to create the universe but accessible enough to become part of His own creation in Jesus Christ. This is why His words are different from all others. These are the words that give us more than blind rules to follow but provide, instead, loving instructions on how to live this life to the fullest. It's the voice that leads us to a narrow path of goodness and light, a voice we can trust because of the life and character that backs it up.

The goal of this book is to build confidence in the reader that Jesus Christ was not only a real person but that He was the promised Messiah (Savior) and the Son of God. It is not my mission to explore every speculation and theory that has attempted to explain away this truth, but to deal with the major obstructions that attempt to block the light that this truth exudes. Without question, the voice you choose to listen to will be the most important decision you will ever make. If you are reading this book, the chances are that you are already a follower of Christ or you desire to explore becoming such a follower. Implicit in that is being able to help others follow Him as well. You have most likely encountered some form of backlash or opposition from others who don't share this same passion and pursuit. Therefore, you want to be able to give them the reasons for your faith. This book is written to be a tool to help you explain and defend the basic truths and claims of the Christian faith—in other words, to answer the Great Question faithfully and truthfully.

Preparing believers to give the reasons for their faith should be the highest priority of all the efforts of those engaged in Christian ministry. After all, if the truth of the message is in doubt, the whole enterprise of Christianity is in jeopardy. As a pastor I certainly am aware of how busy most church leaders are. The demands facing people in ministry to care for the needs of others can be overwhelming. Many times the pressing needs of our people take priority over the pressing questions about the truth of the faith from outsiders. Yet the enormous needs of everyone, everywhere on this planet, have created an opportunity to practically demonstrate God's love and to share the gospel with them. "Be wise in the way you act toward outsiders; make the most of every opportunity. Let your conversation be always full of grace, seasoned with salt, so that you may know how to answer everyone" (Colossians 4:5–6).

Of all the human rights we should be fighting for, leading the way should be the right of every living person to hear the gospel and have the opportunity to know Jesus. While there is amazing work being done around the world by people of faith to help the needy and heal the hurting, we are falling dramatically short in preparing people to have a faith that thrives in the media-saturated, anti-faith twenty-first century. People are flooded with images and messages that suggest faith in God is at best irrelevant. The end result is a large number of Christians being dazed and confused about how crazy the world has become, and how their values and beliefs are not just out of touch with mainstream society but to some are framed as bigoted and ignorant. Perhaps this helps explain why only 3 percent of churches in the United States are growing through evangelism.

The bottom line to me is this simple: if you believe the Jesus story is true and understand why, you will share it with others—if you don't, you won't. Christians must be taught and trained, not just comforted and entertained. Because this type of shallow activity is prevalent, is there any wonder that survey after survey shows the trend that young people are dropping out of church in record numbers?

There is no neutral ground in this debate. The claims about Jesus made in Scripture make it virtually impossible to dismiss Him as just a mere man. The other two options are either myth or Messiah. The choice you make should decide how you operate in every area of your life. If Jesus is a myth, then you should live your life your way. Make up your own morality, be your own boss. But if He is the Messiah, the Lord of creation, then live wholly and holy for Him.

Because Jesus is the source of all goodness and life, then He should be at the very center of our personal lives as well as our culture and practices. To do this, we must recover the confidence that His words are true and can be known with a high degree of certainty. They have not been hopelessly lost due to the passing of hundreds of years and humans trying to put words that He never said into His mouth. Our search for the real Jesus will lead us past all the pretenders who try to claim Him as a part of their stories while dismissing the biggest part of His story—that He is the Lord of all creation. This is vital because the message that Christ offers is hope for humanity. Can you think of anything more needed in our time than that? As Jesus said, "You will know the truth, and the truth will set you free" (John 8:32).

Sometimes a Song Can Get Stuck in Your Head

Such was the case with the world's most famous atheist. During a public discussion at Oxford, with a philosopher and a theologian, Richard Dawkins candidly revealed that he had been singing a hymn that very morning in the shower—one that he had learned as a child in the Anglican Church. It was titled, "It Is a Thing Most Wonderful." After mentioning the title and the first few words of the hymn, he went on to say that, to him, the universe's coming into being out of nothing and then producing beings such as humans with consciousness was simply too wonderful to be.[2] Dawkins obviously stopped short in finishing the rest of the opening stanza of the hymn, words that pointed to another story that was the object of the writer's amazement:

> *It is a thing most wonderful—too wonderful to be*
> *That God's own Son should come from heaven*
> *and die to save a child like me*
> *and yet I know that it is true.*[3]

How ironic that the wonder and grace described in the song was ascribed by Dawkins to simply nothing—nothing but the blind forces of nature. What was missed was the glaring message that Christ was indeed the object of the wonder and the worthy recipient of our gratitude.

You see, like Richard Dawkins, I remember hymns from my childhood as well.

> *We've a story to tell to the nations,*
> *That shall turn their hearts to the right,*
> *A story of truth and mercy,*
> *A story of peace and light.*
> *For the darkness shall turn to dawning,*
> *And the dawning to noonday bright:*
> *And Christ's great kingdom shall come on earth,*
> *The kingdom of love and light.*[4]

It is with this hope that I write. Your answer to the Great Question about Jesus—man, myth, or Messiah?—will be the most important of all. It's an answer worth pursuing with all your heart, mind, soul, and strength. The reality of its truth and power will leave you exclaiming, "It is indeed a thing most wonderful, too wonderful to be."

1

MAN, MYTH, OR MESSIAH?

History's Greatest Question

There is no historical task which so reveals a man's
true self as the writing of a Life of Jesus.[1]
—ALBERT SCHWEITZER

IT'S ONE OF THE STRANGE QUIRKS OF HUMAN NATURE
that we tend to believe wild and absurd things while doubting
and dismissing the credible and important.

This tendency to give credence to foolish and baseless speculations was satirized on the long-running US TV show *Saturday
Night Live*. It ranks as one of my favorite comedy skits of all time.
It was the one where there was an exchange between an angel
and someone who had recently died and gone to heaven. The
new arrival was quizzing the angel on all the unanswered questions and unsolved mysteries of his past existence. The dialogue
went something like this: "What happened to the fifty-dollar

bill I lost at graduation?" and "Who had a crush on me that I didn't know about?" You get the picture. Finally, heaven's newest inductee asked "What is the one thing that would surprise me the most if I knew it?" The character playing the angel dramatically paused and then said, "Professional wrestling is real."[2]

I guess what struck me as funny is that I've actually met people who believed that TV wrestling was authentic (and not staged entertainment); my grandmother was one of them. Of course, there are many people who consider silly things, such as UFOs or Elvis sightings, to be real. As Blaise Pascal wrote in his *Pensées*, "The sensibility of man to trifles, and his insensibility to great things, indicates a strange inversion."[3]

This highlights the tendency to deny events that should be believed, like the Holocaust or Americans walking on the moon and the fact that 9/11 was a terrorist attack carried out by radical Muslims, not a conspiracy of the US government.

Regrettably the amount of misinformation and rumor is rampant in an age where every outlandish viewpoint has its own website and Facebook page. Finding the truth becomes hard work. It also requires our being willing to accept it, regardless of our own personal preferences or biases. In other words, we must be willing to follow the evidence wherever it leads.

While many spurious beliefs are relatively harmless and inconsequential, others could have devastating consequences, especially if real history is obscured or ignored. This was never more obvious to me than when visiting sites like the World War II Nazi concentration camps, such as the one in Auschwitz, Poland. Walking through massive rooms of shoes, suitcases, and hair in what remains of this testimony to hell on earth will dismiss any absurd suggestion that the Holocaust never happened.

Millions of Jews were murdered in one of humankind's darkest moments.

The same can be said of a trip to Yad Vashem, the holocaust memorial in Jerusalem. It is simply outrageous that someone could deny that these unthinkable events did not occur just seventy short years ago.

Forgetfulness of this kind is intentional—a deliberate refusal to remember. This seems to be an all-too-familiar pattern in history. That's because remembering is hard work that requires all our faculties to be unencumbered by bias and personal agendas. These types of painful memories bring us back to the reality of the shameful proclivity in human nature toward cruelty and injustice. If left unchecked and unaccountable, the strong will dominate the weak and helpless, rather than stand up and defend them—especially at the risk of losing our own lives or credibility.

It is because of this fatal flaw in human nature that God sent His own Son in the likeness of humans to walk among us and model the antithesis of this kind of self-centeredness. Jesus Christ lived a life that went against that strong current of history. He lived the life that we should have lived, one that was morally and ethically spotless. No other figure in human history could or would make such a claim to be without sin—Jesus did. For this reason, it was the most unique and important life in history—one we cannot dismiss or ignore.

Yet something so precious and amazing is rejected as an impossibility by skeptics who readily accept absurd and irrational explanations of our existence, especially if they are devoid of any moral implications. They frame all religious beliefs in a one-size-fits-all framework and dismiss it with the charge that faith is blind, or, as they love to say, "faith is believing what you know isn't true."

As atheist writer Michael Shermer states, "Religious faith depends on a host of social, psychological and emotional factors that have little or nothing to do with probabilities, evidence and logic."[4]

Nothing could be further from the truth. While there are many who believe in God without being aware of all the evidence and logic attesting to its truth, this doesn't mean that the evidence and logic don't exist. If you believe in God and are a follower of Christ, that faith is well grounded in history and reason—real faith isn't blind. Yet the Scripture warns, "My people are destroyed for lack of knowledge" (Hosea 4:6 NKJV).

If we desire to not be engulfed by a tsunami of digital absurdity, we must find the solid foundation of something that is true and trustworthy. It's much easier to sit back and flow with what the culture is saying about something rather than sincerely and objectively searching for the truth, regardless of where the evidence may lead.

Every person has the right to know the truth (facts) and make his own decision. With that said, there are definitely pitfalls and dangerous, dark alleys in which you can get mugged and stripped of your faith. It's worth repeating: the voices you listen to in this journey of faith and discovery are critical.

GOD'S NOT DEAD REVISITED

After thirty years of working with university students around the world, I decided to write down the arguments for the existence of God in what I hoped would be a straightforward, concise manner. That effort became the book *God's Not Dead*. It gave a glimpse into the emotionally charged debate that rages between these two opposing views of the world—materialism (atheism) and theism. This is not a friendly discussion. Though there are voices of reason and moderation on both sides, the usual fare is a shouting match of insults rather than arguments, and rhetoric rather than reason. I have been overwhelmed with responses from believers of all ages and backgrounds, who told me the stories of how the voices of intolerance did everything possible to silence their views because they were Christians. They, too, had to take a stand at the risk of losing credibility, grades from a teacher, or even their occupations.

For the follower of Christ, there is a fierce conflict on two distinct fronts. On one side is the challenge we have mentioned of materialism and atheism. The materialist believes that nature is all there is. The world and everything in it can be explained by natural causes with no need for any "supernatural shenanigans," as physicist and atheist Lawrence Krauss puts it.[5] The theistic worldview believes that the order and information in the physical universe point to an intelligent mind behind it all. Information itself is a nonmaterial entity with no mass or physical quality. To the materialist, this defeats the notion that only physical things are real. The nonmaterial nature of information joins the list of other nonphysical realities that scientists depend on to make their hypotheses, observations, measurements, and conclusions. These include mathematics, reason, and the laws of logic. Science itself rests on the assumption that these things are true.

The proponents of the atheistic worldview hope we don't notice that this view doesn't rest on cold, hard facts but rather on a set of presuppositions. It claims to be the worldview endorsed by a majority of the top scientists and thus the only conclusion of the rational and scientifically literate mind. Life is merely a product of random chance and purely natural forces. Since there was no real beginning to humanity, we are just a branch in the evolutionary tree of life; therefore, there is no sin to atone for and no need for a Savior. Life is simply a struggle where the fittest survive. The rest face extinction. We are reduced to being animals programmed by our DNA to survive.

The cloak of academic pretense must be drawn back in order to see the true influence behind this brand of atheism and radical skepticism: the philosophy of naturalism. Contrary to Stephen Hawking's pronouncement that "philosophy is dead,"[6] the writings of the popular atheists demonstrate that bad philosophy is still thriving in the darkness of the unbelieving mind.

The reality is we don't act just like a group of animals struggling to survive. We can think philosophically about the human condition, create ways to remedy injustice wherever it is found, and serve the poor and needy. These actions that help the weak and infirm do not logically follow from an evolutionary instinct or survival point of view. In fact, Darwin said we are hindering the evolutionary process by these acts of inexplicable altruism.[7] Instead, this comes naturally to us because we have been instilled with a moral law that reflects our distinction as humans, made in the image of God. Contrary to Darwin, Jesus said, "Greater love has no one than this: to lay down one's life for one's friends" (John 15:13). This is exactly what Jesus did in laying down His own life to pay for our sins by His death on a Roman cross. He now calls us to love and serve others in His name.

On the other side of the Christian struggle is the challenge that stems from the fact that there are many religions in the world and many contradictory voices describing what God is like and what this God expects of us.

With all the religions in the world, which one is right?

Is it just a matter of sincerity? How can they all be right when, as we shall see, the truth claims of the world's religions are mutually exclusive? In other words, by their own testimonies, they all can't be right. Some believe in one personal God, others in multiple deities, and some in an impersonal force. There are millions of people who will never question what they have been told and blindly follow their cultural beliefs and the faith of their parents. But there are millions more who will examine what they have been told in light of the free market of ideas. They will desire to know what is actually true over what is culturally preferred. That which is really true can withstand the scrutiny of historical, philosophical, and rational inquiry. The very essence of truth is that it is true regardless of culture or context.

God calls us to follow Him with our hearts and minds. We may start out with the faith of our parents, but we must make it our own. Usually this is very hard work. Every religion is based on claims that must be tested in light of history, philosophy, science, and theology. They all make claims that can and should be compared and contrasted. They make claims that can't all be true. For instance, the Koran states that Jesus was not crucified (Sura 4:157–58). The Bible obviously states that not only was He was crucified; He was also raised from the dead. As we will discuss thoroughly in this book, the overwhelming evidence accepted by historians is that Jesus was crucified at the hands of the Roman procurator Pontius Pilate. It doesn't just come down to who can shout the loudest to determine the truth or falsity of the critical statements that the different religions and philosophies make.

We can, and must, be able to make these kinds of clear distinctions between competing claims for truth. The hope from the very beginning of the initial *God's Not Dead* project was to help people fulfill 1 Peter 3:15, "Always be prepared . . . to give the reason for the hope that you have. But do this with gentleness and respect."

A couple of years ago, I took my youngest son, Charlie, on a wilderness journey that was advertised as taking you beyond your comfort zone. He kept telling me, "But I like my comfort zone. Why would I want to get out of it?" There were series of daunting challenges, including a white-water rafting trip. Thankfully, we had a guide on this trip across a series of rapids. Listening to that voice of experience about when to lean left or right, when to paddle, or when to lift our oars out of the water, allowed us to miss a host of dangerous rocks that could have upended us or injured us severely. The people who have injured their faith or lost it altogether because of listening to the wrong voices are too many to count. I am grateful for the mentors I've had that have helped me navigate through the skeptical challenges to the truth of the Christian faith. My hope is to help readers avoid the things that cause a shipwrecking of their trust in God. This starts with accepting a fact that is indeed beyond dispute: Jesus really did exist.

FAITH OR HISTORY?

The fact of Jesus' existence brings the discussion about Him out of the realm of just religious faith into the arena of historical investigation. If someone is intellectually honest, he should at least examine the evidence for His life as he would any other person who lived, such as Socrates, Caesar Augustus, or Napoleon.

The evidence for His life shouldn't be dismissed ahead of time because of the awareness of an extraordinary conclusion, one that might be ominously waiting at the end of the search.

When it comes to Jesus Christ, there has definitely been a higher standard, unreasonably high at times, for establishing the facts surrounding His life, works, and words. The specific criteria used by many modern scholars to verify the authenticity of Jesus have been so demanding that if they were applied to ancient history, most of what is currently accepted would dissolve into oblivion. For instance, imagine asserting, as skeptics do for the biblical records, that we could only know about ancient Rome from what we learn from non-Roman sources. In contrast, scholars who use trusted approaches fairly and consistently recognize that Christian beliefs about Jesus are solidly guarded in historical fact. As stated in *Reinventing Jesus,* "If you are skeptical of the Jesus of the Bible, we hope you'll discover that a step toward him doesn't require leaving your brain behind. If you embrace the biblical Christ but think faith isn't concerned with matters of the mind, we want you to see that belief in the Incarnation—God entering the time-space world as a man two millennia ago—compels you to take history seriously."[8]

Historians use reliable criteria to establish the probability that an event happened in the past. For instance, claims are more likely true if they are reported by multiple, independent sources. By this standard, our knowledge about Jesus is superior to that about virtually every other ancient historical figure. Scholars have discovered more literary sources for the historical Jesus within the first hundred years after His life than all of the primary literary sources for Socrates, which, incidentally, are in far less agreement with each other than the Gospels.[9]

When the historical process is arbitrary and inconsistent, the past becomes something that people with an agenda can manipulate like a fictional story. This type of mind-set leads to the dismissal of the miraculous accounts given by Jesus' followers in the Gospels. Those accounts are replaced with historical profiles of what someone living at the time of Jesus would have *probably* been like. Others go so far as claiming that the followers of Jesus merely borrowed from the mythology of the Egyptians, Greeks, and Persians. The reasoning? The miracles didn't happen because miracles can't happen. We're going to break this down in detail in a later chapter. Pop culture has seized on these unfounded speculations and broadcast them as fact.

Comedian and cultural commentator Bill Maher spews this palaver to the delight of his adoring audiences. Others simply repeat this again and again as if it is part of the creedal orthodoxy of a new skeptical religion. And make no mistake: atheism is a religion. It is a set of beliefs about the nature of the world and about us as humans, and those beliefs have dramatic implications for how we should live and how society should function. At the heart of this anti-theistic system is the necessity to dismiss the supernatural, especially the supernatural birth, life, death, and resurrection of Jesus Christ.

Liar, Lunatic, or Lord?

In an earlier generation the former atheist and legendary author and philosopher C. S. Lewis posed his famous trilemma. He said based on the claims of Jesus in the Gospels about being the Son of God, that He was either a lunatic (because He thought He was God), a liar (because He knew this wasn't true), or He was indeed Lord.

This challenge by Lewis was to help people not get stuck with the position that Jesus was merely a good man and not the Messiah that He claimed and demonstrated Himself to be. Therefore, He was a liar or a lunatic and would be disqualified for being the person we should consider as the ultimate representation of the invisible God.

Bart Erhman, a former evangelical believer turned agnostic who teaches at the University of North Carolina, tells of how he added the word *legend* to the list of options that Lewis proposed when considering the true identity of Jesus. He asked, "What if Jesus didn't claim to be the Son of God?" That would mean that the stories about Christ's miracles and His resurrection from the dead were simply legends, constructed by His followers, long after His death. This notion is echoed by popular writers who dismiss the claim of Jesus being the Christ and relegate Him to being a Jewish zealot who died trying to lead an insurrection against the Romans. Writers, such as Reza Aslan, the sociologist mentioned in the introduction, who turned from the Christian faith back to his original faith of Islam, claim Jesus was an illiterate peasant who never said most of what the Gospels say He said or did the things they say He did. Very little of what Aslan says is original thought however. He simply restates the writings of skeptics before him, such as S. G. F. Brandon, John Dominic Crossan, and Marcus Borg. Aslan ignores the Gospels and opts instead for writings, not about Jesus but about the type of people from His times and from those who might have lived in His town. He asserts, "For better or worse, the only access one can have to the real Jesus comes not from the stories that were told about him after his death, but rather from the smattering of facts we can gather from his life as part of a large Jewish family of woodworkers/builders struggling to survive in the small Galilean village of Nazareth."[10]

That's like saying we can get a better picture of Abraham Lincoln from studying what the people were like in the region of the United States that were his contemporaries rather than studying the accounts of his life from those who knew him best. It is deeply irresponsible to dismiss the testimony as biased from people who believed in Jesus and accept the perceptions of those who didn't believe in Him as more credible.

The growing body of literature making these types of claims, and the rise of Internet skeptics that proclaim this type of writing as "scholarly" and "authoritative," have evoked a renewed effort to set the record straight. That's why the title of this work, *Man, Myth, Messiah*, offers a different trilemma for a different generation.

THE QUEST FOR THE HISTORICAL JESUS

The roots of this culture of skepticism can be traced back to the seventeenth and eighteenth centuries. This period, commonly referred to as the Age of Enlightenment, could better be described as the age of skepticism. The mind-set of this era is summed up by an earlier French mathematician and philosopher named René Descartes. He started with doubt in order to come to a place of confidence about what he could know for sure. "In order to seek truth, it is necessary once in the course of our life, to doubt, as far as possible, of all things."[11]

This perspective left him with the foundation of reality being his own thoughts (albeit doubts) about the fact of his own existence. The seeds that Descartes planted grew over the next century into the Enlightenment era, which heralded that "reason replaced revelation" in terms of the source of the culture's epistemology—that is, how we know what we know.

This philosophical trend blossomed in the nineteenth century with the release of *On the Origin of Species* by Charles Darwin. The theory of evolution by means of natural selection that he described replaced in the minds of skeptics the belief that life needed a designer to account for the "appearance of design in nature." This alternative story radically altered how people would view our origins and by extension our destiny, value, and understanding of ultimate reality. For if there were no need for a supernatural Creator to explain life, then why not dismiss Him altogether?

It should be no surprise that skepticism about the historical Jesus would rise in the same period. If you don't believe in God, or dismiss Him as an impersonal Deity who isn't concerned with the affairs of humans, then you wouldn't believe that He had a Son who was sent to pay for the sins of the world. These doubts about the wonder-working Jesus of Nazareth would be given full expression with liberal theologian David Strauss. His writings cemented a vision of Jesus that would strip away all of the supposed miracles and thus any claim to being the Son of God who died and rose again.

Jesus' identity was further downgraded in 1906 by the book *The Quest of the Historical Jesus* by Albert Schweitzer. He argued that Jesus was not even the great moral instructor envisioned by liberal scholars but simply a well-meaning teacher who was mistaken about the imminent end of the world. Schweitzer also denied most of the New Testament's significant claims about Jesus' life, teachings, and miracles.

> The Jesus of Nazareth who came forward publicly as the Messiah, who preached the ethic of the kingdom of God, who founded the kingdom of heaven upon earth, and died to give his work its final consecration never existed. He is a figure designed by rationalism, endowed with life by liberalism, and clothed by modern theology in a historical garb.
>
> This image has not been destroyed from outside; it has fallen to pieces.[12]

The influence of such scholars is still being felt today. In the twentieth century skeptical theologians and historians continued to build on previous revisions of Jesus and remake Him into everything from an illiterate peasant leading a revolt against Rome to a New Age guru promoting esoteric Eastern mysticism. In the 1980s and '90s, the Jesus Seminar was formed by "a self-selected group of like-minded scholars" as a modern-day tribunal to vote on which words from Scripture they thought Jesus said and which ones were fabricated by later Christians.[13] As you might guess, little remained after their sweeping edits of the Gospels outside some of Jesus' ethical teachings. This effort was reminiscent of Thomas Jefferson, who literally cut out the passages from the Gospels that contained anything supernatural and left only the ethical teachings of Jesus in his own version of the Bible. In the end, most New Testament scholars recognized that the seminar by no means represented the majority of experts in the field but solely the opinion of an extreme faction, many of whom were driven by the desire to discredit historical Christianity.

The Resurrection Changes Everything

The claim that Jesus was resurrected, three days after His death, is not just an article of faith, but it is also a statement that can be examined historically. Philosopher Stephen Davis noted, "I do hold, however, that the meaning of the resurrection depends on the fact of the resurrection. That is, if Jesus was not really raised from the dead, then the resurrection of Jesus has no particularly interesting meaning."[14]

Christianity is based on this central claim and is thus open to critical historical inquiry. In the same way that Charles Darwin in his book *On the Origin of Species* sought to establish the past history of living things through the method called *inference to the best explanation*, we can look at this event using the same process. In fact, the apostle Paul would write that if there were no resurrection, then the Christian faith would be false (1 Corinthians 15:14). Critics have long maintained that religious claims are simply statements of faith without any evidence or substance. Claims of science, they say, are more credible because they can be proven false. Yet this is exactly what Christianity declares. There is no other religion that bases the entire weight of its credibility on a single event or miracle. As stated boldly by Michael Grant, "Christianity is the only religion which stands or falls by supposed historical happenings."[15]

It was this conviction that compelled a small group of Christ followers out of the shadows of fear and unbelief onto the center stage of history. It became the source of a supernatural power and wisdom that would confound their opponents. Ultimately, it would overwhelm an empire, not by military prowess but by heart-piercing truth and relentless love. The world had not witnessed anything like it before or since. Historian Will Durant concludes:

> There is no greater drama in human record than the sight of a few Christians, scorned or oppressed by a succession of emperors, bearing all trials with a fiery tenacity, multiplying quietly, building order while their enemies generated chaos, fighting the sword with the word, brutality with hope, and at last defeating the strongest state that history has ever known. Caesar and Christ had met in the arena, and Christ had won.[16]

It was the belief that Jesus had been raised from the dead that evoked a dedication and sacrifice by His followers to obey His commands. At the top of the list was the command to love their enemies. It is highly unlikely that His followers would have been faithful to those words had Jesus' life ended permanently at the cross. In fact, New Testament scholar N. T. Wright points out that none of the many self-proclaimed messiahs of the ancient world continued to have a following or influence once they died.

One might add, for good measure, the followers not only of John the Baptist but of Judas the Galilean, Simon, Athronges, Eleazar ben Deinaus and Alexander, Menahem, Simon bar Giora, and Bar-Kochba himself. Faced with the defeat of their leader, followers of such figures would either be rounded up or melt away into the undergrowth. The other possibility was to latch onto a new leader. In the case of the apparent dynasty that ended up being known as the Sicarii, when one leader was killed, they simply chose another from the same family. In not one case do we hear of any group, after the death of its leader, claiming that he was in any sense alive again and that, therefore, Israel's expectation had in some strange way actually come true. History, therefore, spotlights this question: What happened to make Jesus' followers, from the very start, articulate such a claim and work out its implications?[17] For us today, the desperate need is to recover the same conviction of the truth of this event that the early disciples possessed.

MORE THAN A HISTORY LESSON

The disciples of Jesus asked the question, "Who is this?" when witnessing Him calming a storm on the Sea of Galilee with the words "Hush, be still." The multitudes asked the same when He rode into Jerusalem a week before His crucifixion to the shouts of "Hosanna" to the King. The answer? He is the Christ—the Messiah.

This belief was certainly grounded in the evidence of the power of His words and His works. He healed the sick, fed the multitudes, walked on water, and even raised Lazarus from the dead. This was no mere man. It would be said that no man spoke the way He spoke (John 7:46). In spite of having this front-row seat to observe the most amazing three years in human history, the disciples of Jesus still grappled with doubt. If they struggled with doubt, having actually seen the miracles unfold before their very eyes, what chance do we have to believe these things two thousand years removed from the original events? This question underscores a key reality when it comes to a relationship with God: there is more to faith than just believing a correct version of history. While the death and resurrection of Jesus are events that can be judged historically, what still remains is an invitation into a relationship that requires a step of faith (trust).

Jesus told Peter after his startling revelation that He was the Christ, "Blessed are you Simon son of Jonah, for this was not revealed to you by flesh and blood, but my Father in heaven" (Matthew 16:17). As the other disciples, Peter had seen the evidence of who Jesus was firsthand. They all saw the same miracles and heard the same words, but they were not able to come to the same conclusion. Something more was needed. The reason lies in the fact that God is not an object to be studied or a force to be measured, but He is personal and, therefore, relational. As in any personal relationship, you cannot force someone to talk to you, much less to give you any deep personal information about himself. Think about your own life. People may know you exist, but that does not mean they can force you to tell them any of your thoughts, feelings, or preferences. In essence, you do not enter into any relationship with someone else without being invited. So it is with God. His Spirit communicates to our hearts the meaning of these facts and then offers us an invitation in the form of promises made. If we believe His words, we will accept His invitation.

Two thousand years after His resurrection, that invitation is still being made, and we can still respond. We can actually have just as fresh an encounter with the Lord as those who walked with Him physically on the shores of Galilee and saw Him after His resurrection. In fact, Jesus told His disciples, "It is for your good that I am going away. Unless I go away, the Advocate will not come to you; but if I go, I will send him to you" (John 16:7). Of course, to suggest that God communicates with humanity directly is to invite deep scorn from the ranks of the unbelieving. Granted, there has been massive abuse in the area of claiming that "God told me" something. Yet such presumption does not mean that God cannot or does not communicate with us. As powerful as the evidence and arguments are for the truth of the Christian faith, the greatest privilege available to humanity is without question a personal relationship with our Creator. As Augustine wrote, "Our hearts are restless until they find their rest in thee."[18] The Scriptures talk about the love of God that "surpasses knowledge" (Ephesians 3:19). Knowing about someone is one thing; knowing him personally is quite another.

Historical evidence can greatly assist people on their journey toward God, but it alone cannot bring a person fully to God. For historians cannot make claims about the ancient past with absolute certainty, only with various levels of confidence. In other words, historians rarely speak in terms of what *definitely* happened but with what *probably* happened, as seen by the following quotation: "No historians really believe in the absolute truth of what they are writing, simply in its probable truth. Notwithstanding, the inability to obtain absolute certainty does not prohibit historians from having adequate certainty."[19]

Said slightly differently, absolute certainty is only possible in such realms as mathematics, but mathematics cannot directly speak to historical events by itself. However, some events are supported by so much evidence that their occurrence is of such high probability that we can, for all practice purposes, say with certainty that they actually occurred. "Mathematical calculations cannot demonstrate the existence and career of Alexander the Great in the fourth century BC. But converging historical evidence would make it absurd to deny that he lived and changed the political and cultural face of the Middle East,"[20] comments author and historian Gerald O'Collins.

The evidence of the resurrection falls into this category. It is so compelling, as determined by the most trustworthy historical standards, that denying the event is unjustifiable, if one truly approaches the evidence objectively and openly. And there lies the challenge. No one is truly objective since all of us view the world through unconscious assumptions and biases. Biases can result from upbringing or other cultural influences. For instance, a person raised to deny the existence of the supernatural would simply dismiss the evidence for the resurrection before even examining it. Biases can also result from people living in rebellion against the true God and giving their hearts to such idols as money, power, and status. As the apostle Paul stated, "The god of this age has blinded the minds of unbelievers, so that they cannot see the light of the gospel that displays the glory of Christ, who is the image of God" (2 Corinthians 4:4).

THE STEP OF TRUST

Regardless of these obstacles, we are given the invitation into a personal relationship with God. It requires a step of trust in the direction the evidence is leading. This step involves both our hearts (spirits) and minds. Remember, the greatest command God gave us was to love Him with all our heart, mind, soul, and strength (Mark 12:29–30; Deuteronomy 6:4–5). And Jesus taught, "God is spirit, and those who worship Him must worship in spirit and truth" (John 4:24 NKJV).

If we worshipped God with only our minds, we would be left with merely an intellectual exercise, limited by our own intellectual abilities and capacity. In contrast, true love goes well beyond just the intellect. Anyone who is married or in love can testify of the transcendental nature of loving someone else. It is an experience that includes analysis and cognition, but that is only one dimension. We are spiritual beings, not just physical. However, the mind is still essential. The intellectual dimension acts as a judge and arbiter of the facts available to us. We need to believe in our hearts but not dismiss our minds, for it is not either/or. Such a false choice is the constant refrain of skeptics that faith and reason are irreconcilable. Yet the two are not only compatible but inseparably linked.

God has made us in such a way that we can grasp something with our hearts (spirits) even if our minds cannot fully comprehend it. How can the finite fully grasp the infinite? If there is a central message of Scripture, from beginning to end, it is trust. God gives us enough evidence in the things we can know, to trust Him in the things that we are not capable of understanding.

As a father of five children, I have spent many days teaching them to trust me. When they were learning to swim, I would ask them to jump into my arms from the side of the pool while I stood in the water. They did not understand all the reasons why I could or should be trusted when I asked them to take a "leap of faith," but they had enough evidence to trust my words anyway and jump. I was actually asking them to take a step of trust. My request to my children is similar to the step of trust God asks of us. He calls us to believe in Him, not based on blind faith but on how He has proven Himself trustworthy both in our lives and throughout history.

SUMMARY

When it comes to the central issues of the Christian faith, the biggest dispute is usually not with the facts of history but with the presuppositions and worldviews of those who interpret those facts. As you hear and weigh the evidence about Jesus, you will be able to know with confidence that He is the Son of God. Chapters 2 through 5 will demonstrate that overwhelming evidence validates that Jesus was truly a man of history, who was crucified, dead, buried, and then rose from the dead. In addition, these chapters defend that the Gospels are reliable accounts of Jesus' life, ministry, and teaching. Chapter 6 will dismiss the absurd notion that Jesus' life was rooted in pagan mythology. Chapter 7 will then demonstrate that Jesus was the promised Messiah, who is the Savior of the world. Chapter 8 will continue this theme by defending the reality of Jesus' miracles, and it will demonstrate that His followers continued to perform miracles in His name after His resurrection until this very day. Finally, chapters 9 and 10 will explain how you can come to know Jesus personally and then step into His purposes for your life.

2

THE MINIMAL FACTS

What Even Skeptics Believe

Habermas has compiled a list of more than 2,200
sources in French, German, and English in which
experts have written on the resurrection from 1975 to
the present. He has identified minimal facts that are
strongly evidenced and which are regarded as historical
by a large majority of scholars, including skeptics.[1]
—MICHAEL LICONA

AS A YOUNG DOCTORAL STUDENT AT MICHIGAN STATE
University, Gary Habermas was losing his Christian faith. It's
not uncommon to hear of these types of stories, as people wade
through the volumes of debate and critical speculation surrounding belief in the Scriptures as God's revealed Word to humanity.
Gary was so shaken and exhausted from this enterprise that he
contemplated becoming a Buddhist. He had read in the Bible
how the apostle Paul said that if Christ was not raised from the
dead, then Christianity was false—or as he said it, "your faith is

futile" (1 Corinthians 15:17). He concluded from this that if he could have confidence that the resurrection really took place, that knowledge would save his faith. He then proposed to his doctoral committee that he desired to write on the resurrection of Jesus. The committee consisted of a Jewish scholar, an agnostic, and two others who did not believe the Scriptures were the inspired Word of God. The leader said, "That's fine; just don't come back and tell us that Jesus was raised from the dead just because the Bible says so."

As he researched the historical evidence for the resurrection, he assembled the facts that a majority of historians would accept, regardless of whether they were Christian, agnostic, or atheist. He would come to call this method the "minimal facts" approach.[2] It is well designed for discussing the faith with skeptics and doubters, since it shows that Christian beliefs, particularly the resurrection, are not just an issue of faith, but a question of history.

Dr. Michael Licona, a historian and an advocate for the minimal facts approach, says, "Some facts are so strongly evidenced that they are virtually indisputable. These facts are referred to as 'historical bedrock.' . . . Historical bedrock includes those facts that meet two criteria. First, they are so strongly evidenced that the historian can fairly regard them as historical facts. Second, the majority of contemporary scholars regard them as historical facts."[3] The specific types of evidence, which lead to the designation of a historical fact, fall into several categories. As mentioned previously, a historical claim is typically considered highly probable if it is made by multiple independent sources. Paul Maier states, "Many facts from antiquity rest on just one ancient source, while two or three sources in agreement generally render the fact unimpeachable."[4]

In addition, sources are considered more reliable if they originate shortly after the actual events. Furthermore, texts are regarded as more trustworthy if they record details that are actually embarrassing to the authors. The more of these criteria that historical data meet, the more likely a historical claim will become recognized as a fact.

The process of evaluating historical claims by these criteria is, in essence, the scientific method applied to history. The minimal facts approach provides common ground to engage people in a meaningful discussion. For me, someone who firmly believes in the reliability of Scripture, this approach was truly a breakthrough in terms of communicating the truth of the gospel to unbelievers, who doubted the reliability of the Gospels.

It also serves as a tool for dealing with radical skeptics who would not engage in the real evidence for the Christian faith and simply assert such absurdities as Jesus did not exist. Their approach could be called "blind doubt." Such skepticism could never be used by historians of ancient history without undermining the entire discipline. "If we started with the default skepticism toward other ancient sources that some scholars place on the Gospels, we would know quite little about antiquity."[5]

Facts are pesky things. They tend to get in the way of an opponent's assertion that there is no evidence that Christianity is true. In this chapter we examine some of the many facts of history that scholars such as Habermas have set forth as minimal facts. These include events mentioned both outside the Scripture as well as within. Remember, even the most ardent skeptics accept many things in the Bible as true.

Before we get into the minimal facts, we examine the most obvious claim of the Christian faith that some have called into question, "Did Jesus really exist?" Jesus' existence is not listed as a minimal fact for the obvious reason—of course He existed.

However, because there are those who want to challenge this fact in order to make the arguments moot about what He said, what He did, and who He really was, we start our discussion at this elementary level.

BREAKING NEWS: JESUS LIVED!

Up until the last few years, the verdict of historians has been virtually unanimous that Jesus was a person of history. The rise of atheism in the last decade has seen the rise of prominent skeptics who simply assert their "doubts" that Jesus really existed without providing any credible evidence. I've heard prominent atheists, such as Richard Dawkins and others, say things like, "Jesus, if He even existed, . . ." It's important to note that these men are not historians and simply assert this contention in apparent hopes that no one will challenge them because they are scientists. Dawkins has since recanted and admits Jesus existed.[6]

This dismissive attitude, however, has seeped into the bloodstream of pop culture as well and thrives in the blogosphere and on atheist websites. It is the equivalent of getting your news from a tabloid at the grocery store—the kind with a headline like "I Was Abducted by Aliens." One of the leading skeptical voices, Bart Erhman, noted, "Jesus existed, and those vocal persons who deny it do so not because they have considered the evidence with the dispassionate eye of the historian, but because they have some other agenda that this denial serves."[7]

This fact of history is settled in the minds of serious historians, regardless of their religious beliefs. Jesus' life of approximately thirty-three years is still the most important one in all of human existence. His teachings are the bedrock of civilization two thousand years later.

Even the necessity of defending the fact that Jesus was a real person demonstrates the nature of the challenge of living in an age where information quickly mutates into disinformation. Radical deniers disavow any event that does not fit their preferred narrative. To the skeptic desperately trying to shout down any suggestion of the historical credibility of the Christian faith, Jesus' actual existence is a difficult impossible concession to make.

There is a bit of irony that I am writing this chapter while in Jerusalem. It would be difficult to find anyone living here today who would deny that Jesus existed. The impact of His life on this land is undeniable. Multitudes pour into this part of the world to be given extensive tours of the places where Jesus lived, preached, and worked miracles. It's long been my sense that anyone doubting Jesus' existence should simply come to Israel and take a one-week tour. And you don't need a scholar or historian. Any tour guide can set you straight. Yet to some, especially those under thirty in the United States, this has become a point of uncertainty.

Recently I was sitting in a meeting with one of the leading youth communicators in America, Heath Adamson. He paused after hearing the discussion on my writing a book that tells that Jesus existed and said, "This is the most important question we can answer for young people struggling to find faith—did Jesus really exist?" If Jesus never lived, then this whole thing about faith in Him is a sham.

On the surface, the motivation of such blind doubt is obvious. If Jesus never existed, then you don't have to bother with all the hard work of looking at the evidence of His words or His works or all the other historical facts that demand a fair hearing.

Just like the debate surrounding the existence of God, the skeptics think that by repeating the magic phrase over and over, "there is no evidence for God . . . there is no evidence for God," all of it will simply disappear. They seem to be trying the same trick when it comes to the existence of Jesus Christ.

In the movie *God's Not Dead 2*, the debate rages over whether a teacher can even mention the name of Jesus in a classroom. If Jesus lived, why shouldn't He be referenced, especially in view of the fact that the impact of His life is still being felt today? Even His critics concede that His words changed the world and gave us an ethical standard unmatched in history. William Lecky was not a friend of Christians; he was an opponent who wrote,

> Christianity following its leader has shown itself capable of acting on all ages, nations, temperaments, and conditions, has been not only the highest pattern of virtue, but also the strongest incentive to its practice, and has exercised so deep an influence that it may be truly said that the simple record of three short years of active life has done more to regenerate and soften mankind than all the disquisitions of philosophers and all the exhortation of moralists.[8]

The real motivation for skeptics to deny that Jesus really lived is not a lack of evidence. They often desire to attack Christianity in any way possible because of the evil perpetrated by self-proclaimed Christians. Sadly, this perspective represents a tragic misunderstanding of history and Scripture. The dark actions done in Jesus' name, atrocities during the Crusades, the Inquisition, attacks against the Jewish people, have all come in direct opposition to His words. He even predicted that many would call Him "Lord, Lord," but they would not do what He said (Luke 6:46).

Furthermore, many of the followers of Jesus would eventually be put to death rather than deny that He lived, died, and rose again. What could people possibly have gained from fabricating a teaching that included "loving your enemies" and "the greatest among you will be your servant"?

The religious leaders certainly would not have fabricated a character that called them out for their hypocrisy. The Roman rulers couldn't have been the source of this story either—they wanted no challenges to their authority. No, the evidence is abundantly clear. The Jesus of history is indeed the Christ of faith recorded in Scripture. The vital first step is to know what that historical evidence is. In doing so, you will be prepared to handle the baseless assertions that circulate in our culture with the intent to undermine faith in the credibility of the Christian story.

Remember, we are looking for the evidence of history accepted even by those who do not trust the overall reliability of the Gospels. As we will see clearly in chapter 3, the Gospels are reliable and are excellent sources for establishing what happened historically in terms of the life of Jesus. However, to meet the skeptics on their terms and look at evidence accepted by most historians, we can still establish the following events and claims as true.

He Was Crucified

The first minimal fact is that Jesus died by crucifixion. The cross is the symbol of the Christian faith and without question the most recognizable religious emblem in the world. Almost two billion people believe that Jesus' crucifixion had something to do with their sins being absolved by God. In the next chapter, we look deeper into the reasons why He was crucified and how His death affects our relationship with God. Here, we look at the fact that His execution really happened. Not only do all four gospels report it, but virtually all early church writings are filled with references to this event.

On top of this evidence are the records by historians and writers who were not sympathetic to the Christian cause. When an enemy or opponent references an event, historians count that fact as a mark of authenticity. The most famous Jewish source is Flavius Josephus, a Jewish historian who was employed by the Romans and wrote during the time of Christ. He would write, "When Pilate, upon hearing him accused by men of the highest standing amongst us, had condemned him to be crucified . . ."[9]

A second source is Tacitus, who is generally regarded as the greatest of the Roman historians. He was the proconsul of Asia from AD 112 to 113. His last work, *The Annals*, was written circa AD 116–117 and included, "Nero fastened the guilt [of the burning of Rome] and inflicted the most exquisite tortures on a class hated for their abominations, called Christians by the populace. Christus, from whom the name had its origin, suffered the extreme penalty during the reign of Tiberius at the hands of one of our procurators, Pontius Pilatus."[10]

Another Roman source was Lucian. He was a second-century playwright who wrote, "The Christians, you know, worship a man to this day—the distinguished personage who introduced their novel rites, and was crucified on that account."[11]

As a final example, the collection of Jewish teaching known

as the Talmud reports that "on the eve of the Passover, *Yeshua* was hanged."[12] *Yeshua* is "Joshua" in Hebrew (translated "Jesus" in Greek). Being hung on a tree was used to describe crucifixion in antiquity.

The entire saga of Jesus' trial, execution, and the scattering of His disciples left a crater in history that bears witness to the reality of these fateful events. Jesus' death by crucifixion is a historical fact supported by considerable evidence. In fact, on the continuum of historical probability, Jesus' crucifixion "under Pontius Pilate" is the most certain of all claims related to Jesus.[13]

His Tomb Was Found Empty

Another important fact is that after Jesus' crucifixion, His tomb was found empty by a group of His women followers. The empty tomb is not technically included by Habermas as a minimal fact, since the number of critical scholars who accept it drops to around 75 percent[14] (compared to more than 90 percent for the other minimal facts[15]). This drop is likely due to the profound implication of an empty tomb. If Jesus were buried after His death, then the empty tomb would be a decisive additional piece of evidence for the disciples encountering a physical Jesus.

Despite the slightly lower acceptance, the evidence for an empty tomb is enormous. First, all four gospels mention that women were the first eyewitnesses. This fact is significant because the testimony of women was usually dismissed in ancient trials.[16] So no first-century author would have ever made the story up.

All four gospels also specifically mention that the body of Jesus was immediately requested from Pilate by Joseph of Arimathea, and he placed it in his tomb. In addition, the early creed that Paul mentioned in 1 Corinthians 15:4 says, "He was buried." If He was buried, then the tomb would have been a geographical, as well as historical, marker. All that the Roman and Jewish authorities would have had to do was produce the dead body of Jesus and the Christian story would have come to a screeching halt.

Skeptics attempt to work around this evidence by asserting that Jesus would not have received a proper burial. Rather, the Romans would have thrown His body to the wild animals. First of all, such an act would have violated the Roman laws, which stated that the customs of those nations they occupied should be respected as much as possible.[17] Such laws were enacted in order to keep the peace.[18] In addition, Jewish law expressly commanded bodies of the condemned be buried so that the land would not be defiled. "If someone guilty of a capital offense is put to death and their body is exposed on a pole, you must not leave the body hanging on the pole overnight. Be sure to bury it that same day, because anyone who is hung on a pole is under God's curse. You must not desecrate the land the LORD your God is giving you as an inheritance" (Deuteronomy 21:22–23).

As New Testament scholar Craig Evans stated, "Given Jewish sensitivities and customs, burial would have been expected, even demanded."[19] Equally significant, early church tradition is unanimous in its designation of the site of the tomb. And the identified site is within the walls of Jerusalem, after they were repositioned further outward between AD 41 and 43. Custom required Jesus to be buried outside the walls, so the tradition for the site's location had to go back to within ten years of the resurrection. The likelihood of a story of a tomb being fabricated so close to the actual events is remote.[20] Such overwhelming cumulative evidence indicates that the skepticism of those who deny the burial and the empty tomb is without any solid historical foundation.

His Disciples Believed He Appeared to Them

The third minimal fact is the disciples' experiences of the risen Jesus. The evidence supporting this fact is on par with that for Jesus' crucifixion. How historians are willing to explain those appearances is a different question. While skeptics won't acknowledge a real resurrection or a bodily appearance, they concede that it is a fact that His disciples and skeptics, such as Paul (who was a persecutor) and James (Jesus' brother), believed that He appeared to them after His death. Luke Timothy Johnson, in his book, *The Writing of the New Testament*, stated:

> *Something happened* in the lives of real women and men; something that caused them to perceive their lives in a new and radically altered fashion. . . . If we grant that something happened, however, then we must face the still harder question, what happened? What could be profound enough and powerful enough to change timorous followers into bold and prophetic leaders? What power could transform a fanatic persecutor into a fervent apostle?[21]

One of the strongest pieces of evidence for this conclusion comes from Paul's recounting what he heard about the appearances from eyewitnesses. Scholars widely accept that Paul was the author of the book of Galatians, where he described how he had seen the Lord on the road to Damascus, then three years later went to Jerusalem and talked to Peter and James. From these encounters Paul details the appearances in 1 Corinthians 15:3–8:

For what I received I passed on to you as of first importance: that Christ died for our sins according to the Scriptures, that he was buried, that he was raised on the third day according to the Scriptures, and that he appeared to Cephas [Peter], and then to the Twelve. After that, he appeared to more than five hundred of the brothers and sisters at the same time, most of whom are still living, though some have fallen asleep. Then he appeared to James, then to all the apostles, and last of all he appeared to me also, as to one abnormally born.

Paul outlines a credible list of the key eyewitnesses who bore witness to the reality that Jesus had risen from the dead.

Another significant indication of the fact that the disciples believed they had seen the risen Jesus was the transformation of their lives and their character. For instance, James, Jesus' half brother, was not a follower during His initial ministry. In fact, he was a skeptic and a critic along with the rest of Jesus' family (Mark 3:21; John 7:5). After seeing Jesus alive, he became a leader of the early church in Jerusalem, and he was eventually stoned to death, as recorded by the historian Josephus.[22] The other disciples also turned from disillusioned doubters to bold proclaimers of the resurrection. In fact, they all were willing to suffer and die for their conviction that Jesus rose from the grave. And we have good evidence that some were even martyred.[23]

There are accounts of others who claimed to be the Messiah, but their deaths would quickly scatter their followers and end their movements. Such an example was referred to in Acts 5:34–39, when the religious leaders were confronted by the news of Jesus being alive. The fact that the movement grew by hundreds of people, based on testimony that Jesus was alive, demonstrates the most logical conclusion is the claimed appearances were genuine.

The Gospels provide an additional layer of support. Matthew and Luke record Jesus' appearing to the disciples after His resurrection in Galilee:

> Then the eleven disciples went to Galilee, to the mountain where Jesus had told them to go. When they saw him, they worshiped him; but some doubted. Then Jesus came to them and said, "All authority in heaven and on earth has been given to me. Therefore go and make disciples of all nations, baptizing them in the name of the Father and of the Son and of the Holy Spirit." (Matthew 28:16–19)

John also describes several appearances, and the likely original ending of Mark mentions that they would soon take place (Mark 16:7). Skeptics might not accept the exact details of the appearance narratives. Nor would they concede that Jesus was really physically present. However, the majority of leading scholars would acknowledge that their inclusion in multiple, independent sources, including those for the Gospels and the apostle Paul, indicates that appearances of some sort actually took place.

Additional evidence comes from the sermon and speech summaries found in the book of Acts. As a caveat, many scholars would not accept Acts as historically reliable, so it would not technically be part of a minimal-facts argument. However, the following chapter demonstrates that an honest evaluation of the book strongly supports it as a trustworthy source. In particular, a historian of Luke's caliber would have faithfully represented the speakers' original content.[24] And Luke (the author) had access to eyewitnesses and other very early sources. Acts specifically mentions that Luke was a traveling companion of Paul, and he accompanied him to Jerusalem and met with James and the elders (Acts 21:18). Therefore, the summaries represent solid evidence for the apostles testifying to the appearances.

For instance, Peter mentions them in his message to the first Gentile believers:

"We are witnesses of everything he did in the country of the Jews and in Jerusalem. They killed him by hanging him on a cross, but God raised him from the dead on the third day and caused him to be seen. He was not seen by all the people, but by witnesses whom God had already chosen—by us who ate and drank with him after he rose from the dead." (Acts 10:39–41)

They are also described in the message Paul gave on his first missionary journey to a Jewish synagogue:

"Though they found no proper ground for a death sentence, they asked Pilate to have him executed. When they had carried out all that was written about him, they took him down from the cross and laid him in a tomb. But God raised him from the dead, and for many days he was seen by those who had traveled with him from Galilee to Jerusalem. They are now his witnesses to our people." (Acts 13:28–31)

Several other examples could be added to demonstrate that the apostles included the appearances as a central part of their witness.

Proclaimed Early

A fourth minimal fact is the resurrection was proclaimed very early (just days after the actual event). Christianity started in the place where it was least likely to succeed, where it would have been easiest to disprove—Jerusalem three days after His death. Even though leading skeptical scholars admit that the resurrection of Jesus was proclaimed very early, professional skeptics often attempt to obscure or even deny this fact—obviously because of the implications. Rather than engage in historical debate, works of popular fiction like *The Da Vinci Code* make claims that Christianity came to prominence because of Constantine in AD 325. The reality is that the preaching of the resurrection turned the world upside down, from the very beginning. As was mentioned, 1 Corinthians 15:3–8 represents an early creed that Paul received from Peter *fewer than five years after* Jesus' death during his early visit to Jerusalem. Since creeds require time to become standardized, the original teaching had to have originated years earlier.[25]

Moreover, the death, burial, and resurrection are also mentioned in Acts as part of the earliest sermons. The evidence from Acts is significant, but to keep within the minimal-facts criteria, it will be classified as supplementary for the same reasons as mentioned above. In addition, early key church fathers, such as Polycarp, Ignatius, and Papias, wrote about the early beginnings of the faith and the resurrection's central importance. These sources are discussed in greater detail in chapter 3.

This evidence makes the early proclamation of the gospel a historical fact, which is recognized by virtually all New Testament scholars. Even Bart Ehrman dates the preaching of the resurrection to within two years of the event. James Dunn, one of the world's foremost scholars, dates it to within months of the tomb. And Larry Hurtado, a pioneer in the study of the early church, dates the preaching to within days of the events.[26] Therefore, the Christian message is not based on a myth that developed over years within the church. Nor is it based on some corporate self-delusion triggered by the disciples' grief over having lost their beloved leader; such a scenario would have required a much longer period of time to develop. The early proclamation that Jesus of Nazareth had been raised from the dead and, therefore, was the promised Messiah began very soon after His death, and only this message could have produced in so short a time congregations of faithful believers all around the Mediterranean world.

Saul of Tarsus

Fifthly, historians are virtually unanimous in their belief that Saul of Tarsus, also known as Paul, was a harsh opponent of the new sect of Judaism called Christianity, but he was transformed into a defender of the faith after he believed he encountered the risen Jesus. Scholars also accept that he wrote at least seven of the New Testament epistles (letters) that bear his name. One of his greatest contributions was to interact with eyewitnesses of Jesus' ministry and pass their testimonies on to us (1 Corinthians 15, Galatians 1 and 2). He described how he met James, the brother of Jesus; John; and Peter, where "I presented to them the gospel that I preach" (Galatians 2:2). Bart Ehrman talks about Paul spending fifteen days with Peter (Galatians 1:18). Ehrman, as any other person interested in Christianity, says he would have loved to have spent fifteen days with Peter.

So why do historians indicate that they accept Paul's testimony as a part of the historical bedrock? First, as we just mentioned, Paul provides us with his own eyewitness report. The fact that he saw the risen Christ was not only written by Paul himself, but Luke, a historian and his traveling companion, wrote about his dramatic encounter in the book of Acts (Acts 9:27). Second, he was originally a violent enemy of the Christian movement, so historians give more weight to his statements concerning the events he reported. There was no greater enemy to the young movement than him. Imagine someone like Richard Dawkins being converted and becoming a champion for Christ. That was the magnitude of Saul's salvation. Third, he provided embarrassing testimony about himself and the total reversal of his determined actions. Admitting that he was wrong in light of his tireless efforts to discredit and destroy Christianity is considered highly credible evidence. Fourth, he was highly educated, and he wrote in detail about his encounter with the risen Christ and his subsequent transformation (Galatians 1–2). Finally, he was willing to suffer and die for the Christian movement he had previously persecuted. He was martyred by Nero in AD 64.[27]

Imagine Saul, a Roman citizen, willfully submitting to forgo an advantage that status gave him and volunteering to suffer the ultimate punishment of the death penalty all because he refused to deny that Jesus was indeed raised from the dead and, therefore, the promised Messiah. "This point is well documented, reported by Paul himself, as well as Luke, Clement of Rome, Polycarp, Tertullian, Dionysius of Corinth, and Origen. Therefore, we have early, multiple, and firsthand testimony that Paul converted from being a staunch opponent of Christianity to one of its greatest proponents."[28]

All of this evidence points to the conclusion that Saul was transformed because he believed he had seen the risen Jesus.

OTHER MINIMAL FACTS

We outlined the five minimal facts most commonly used to defend the resurrection. However, there are many more that the majority of scholars would accept. I will mention briefly two additional minimal facts and one strongly supported event, but I go into greater detail about them throughout the remaining chapters.

James the Skeptic Became a Disciple of Jesus

The first additional minimal fact is that James, the half brother of Jesus, was originally a skeptic and critic of his brother's ministry (Mark 3:20–21; John 7:1–5). However, he would later come to believe that Jesus was the Son of God, after he saw Him alive following His death. The appearance to James was mentioned in the 1 Corinthians 15 creed. James would also later become the leader of the church in Jerusalem (Acts 15:13–21). And he was martyred by Jerusalem's religious leaders, as recorded by Eusebius and Josephus.[29] Something extraordinary had to occur to convince a skeptic that his brother was the Savior of the world.

The Christian Church Was Established and Grew

The second additional minimal fact relates to the sudden beginning and growth of the Christian church. Virtually all scholars agree that the church was immediately established in Jerusalem and grew quickly. Evidence from Paul's letters indicates that substantial Christian churches had been established throughout the Roman Empire, from Judea to Greece to Rome, within a few decades of the crucifixion. The early expansion is also confirmed by the writings of Roman leaders and historians, such as Pliny the Younger, Suetonius, Tacitus, and even the Jewish Talmud. The authors would not have taken notice of the early Christians until their numbers became significant.

John the Baptist Baptized Jesus

The final event supported by significant historical evidence is John the Baptist baptizing Jesus.[30] John is mentioned in all four gospel accounts. The actual baptism is mentioned in the gospels of Mark, Matthew, and Luke (Mark 1:9–11; Matthew 3:13–17; Luke 3:21–22), and the gospel of John implies that it had taken place (John 1:29–34). All of the gospels also describe supernatural confirmations of Jesus' ministry. In addition, John was baptizing people for the forgiveness of sins. So his baptizing Jesus could imply that Jesus was inferior to John, which would have been embarrassing for the early church. As such, the story would not likely have been made up. These facts have convinced even liberal scholars that the event is historical.[31]

SUMMARY

I remember hearing that there were certain facts about the life and death of Jesus as well as subsequent events after His death that were considered facts of history, even by skeptics. Though I believed the stories in the Bible were true, I struggled at times in communicating those facts effectively to unbelievers who dismissed my use of Scripture. The minimal facts approach, as taught by Dr. Habermas, helped me to coalesce those key events and present them clearly to others. This approach was an enormous confidence builder for my own faith, and I hope that you will master it to solidify your faith and more effectively communicate it to others.

3

WE CAN TRUST
THE GOSPELS

Why the Bible Is Reliable

*A man whose accuracy can be demonstrated in matters
where we are able to test it is likely to be accurate even
where the means for testing him are not available. Accuracy
is a habit of mind, and we know from happy experience
that some people are habitually accurate just as others can
be depended upon to be inaccurate. Luke's record entitles
him to be regarded as a writer of habitual accuracy.*[1]
—F. F. BRUCE

LOTS OF SONS THINK THEIR FATHERS ARE HEROES.
I definitely do. As a young man, my father, Bill Broocks, served
in the navy during World War II, on a submarine called the
USS *Barb*. Because of the bold and daring acts during numerous
conflicts at sea, the admiral of the ship received the Congressional
Medal of Honor. Fittingly, all the crew deserved and received
recognition as a result.

Dad can still recount many of the events of seventy years ago quite vividly. For him, it was a roughly three-and-a-half year period that was unforgettable. I sat and listened as he—in his late eighties—told stories of some of the exploits they participated in and the grave challenges they faced. His older brother, Ben, was a marine and was killed on the island of Saipan when a suicide bomber jumped into his bunker, killing himself and many others in the vicinity. My dad got the news while the *Barb* was in port at Pearl Harbor. The admiral took my dad to the island of Saipan, with a conflict still raging there, and allowed him and two friends to row a small boat to shore and then crawl through a dark cemetery for several hours to locate his brother's grave so his body could be returned to the United States for a proper burial. They only had the light of the moon, intermittently shining through the clouds to guide them. What was stunning to me about that story is that he waited so long to tell us the details. He was from a different generation, to be sure. Many have called it "the greatest generation."

When hearing these stories recounted from seventy years ago, I was reminded of the apostle John, who was part of another unforgettable three-and-a-half-year campaign. He was an eyewitness to the heroic acts and ministry of Jesus of Nazareth. He would write his accounts of these events about sixty-five to seventy years later. Listening to how clear my dad's memory was about the notable incidents of the war showed me how realistic it is to recall the past, especially events that had a dramatic impact on many people.

The writers of the other gospels, Mark, Luke, and Matthew, would write even earlier, as we will discuss shortly. Mark wrote his gospel about thirty to forty years, at the latest, after the death and resurrection of Jesus. That would be like my trying to recall the events of 1981, the year an assassination attempt was made on Ronald Reagan. Matthew and Luke would write about fifty years later, which would be like trying to remember the turbulent times of the 1960s.

However, the gospel writers were not simply writing down events from distant memory. They had access to other leaders and members of the church who had repeated the stories again and again for decades, and they drew from other written records. Each gospel author wrote an authoritative compilation, in his own style, of Jesus' life, teaching, and ministry, which had been faithfully remembered and passed on from the very beginning.

The Gospels Under the Microscope

The four accounts of Jesus' life, death, and resurrection are arguably the most read, studied, scrutinized, and yet beloved literature in history. They have been the subject of countless cover stories, books, papers, and even revisionist books and movies. The described time frames and analogies are very important in the discussion of the reliability of these testimonies about Jesus Christ. The skeptical narrative asserts that the Gospels were written too long after the actual events to be reliable, and they were merely creative expressions of faith by the young community of believers. However, such depictions deny much of the evidence from history and archaeology.

The primary reason many dismiss the Gospels is because they reject the possibility of any supernatural events or miracles. This mind-set was rooted in nineteenth-century German liberalism and skepticism, which imbibed this kind of naturalistic philosophy. If you reject a prioi all things supernatural as myth or legend, then you will reject many occurrences of these types in the New Testament. These attacks do not represent the objective conclusions of scholars carefully examining the facts. Instead, they are often the attempts of men and women to reject the consequences of acknowledging the authority that Jesus' teaching should hold over their lives. In other words, they begin their studies assuming that the Gospels are false and then force the evidence to fit their predetermined conclusions.

Others were raised with an improper understanding of the writing styles of the time, so they fail to appreciate the flexibility first-century authors had to record events and teaching in their own words or to rearrange material. They then consider the differences between parallel accounts in the Gospels as "contradictions" or "errors" that undermine their reliability. This chapter will demonstrate that fairly examining the evidence with a proper understanding of first-century literature leads to the conclusion that the Gospels represent reliable history.

To bolster that trust, we examine several key questions, the answers for which will, hopefully, build greater confidence in the reliability of Scripture.

What Are the Gospels?

The Gospels are now recognized by scholars as historical biographies, the same type that would have been common in the Greek and Roman world two thousand years ago. This style of writing was not a daily chronological account of someone's life but an arrangement by the writer of the details that seemed most important in making the overall moral lessons clearer. The fact that they are biographies dismisses the speculation that these writings were in the form of legends or myths. Historian Michael Licona affirms the significance of this conclusion: "The very fact that they chose to adapt Greco-Roman biographical conventions to tell the story of Jesus indicated that they were centrally concerned to communicate what they thought really happened."[2]

Skeptics desperately want to deny the Gospels are giving historical data. The reason? Because what's at stake is the authority of Jesus in our lives and culture. They attack their reliability by attempting to reduce them to statements of faith by Christians long after the events took place. A prime example is Reza Aslan, who wrote, "Regardless, the gospels are not, nor were they ever meant to be, a historical documentation of Jesus's life. These are not eyewitness accounts of Jesus's words and deeds recorded by people who knew him. They are testimonies of faith composed by communities of faith and written many years after the events they describe. Simply put, the gospels tell us about Jesus the Christ, not Jesus the man."[3]

These kinds of statements are simply repetitions of the same empty assertions of other skeptics before them, desperate to reduce Jesus down to the level of another man who failed in His Quixote-like quest. If you throw out the Gospels, you are free to interpret what they really meant from a quasi-historical standpoint, drawing a sketch of Jesus based on your imagination of what someone living at the time of Jesus would have been like. This is the fatal flaw in both the historiography as well as the logic of the skeptical mind. In contrast, scholars who honestly compare the Gospels to the literature of the day recognize that these writings represent biographies based on eyewitness testimony, which faithfully document Jesus' life, ministry, and most importantly, His resurrection.

Who Wrote the Gospels and When?

The names Matthew, Mark, Luke, and John are probably the most famous quartet of authors in history. You know someone is famous when you don't need a last name to know who he is. The fact that they were the authentic authors of these biographies of Jesus has been accepted since the very beginning of the Christian faith. However, during the past few centuries, skeptics have questioned the traditionally assigned authorship as a strategy to dismiss the authority of their content. Skeptics instead argue that the true authors did not have access to eyewitnesses, so their accounts are unreliable. However, the evidence for the traditional authorship is still very compelling.[4]

Major scholarly works have been written on this topic. The goal here is to provide a brief summary of the evidence for the authorship of these critical books. The strongest evidence for the traditional view is that the testimony of early church leaders is nearly uniform on who wrote each book. For instance, a prominent second-century bishop named Irenaeus quoted several details about the gospel authors from an early-second-century source, a bishop named Papias, who studied under the apostle John:

> Matthew also issued a written Gospel among the Hebrews in their own dialect, while Peter and Paul were preaching at Rome, and laying the foundations of the Church. After their departure, Mark, the disciple and interpreter of Peter, did also hand down to us in writing what had been preached by Peter. Luke also, the companion of Paul, recorded in a book

the Gospel preached by him. Afterwards, John, the disciple of
the Lord, who also had leaned upon His breast, did himself
publish a Gospel during his residence at Ephesus in Asia.[5]

Mark

The first gospel to be written was by Mark, which is commonly
dated between AD 60 and 70. Mark was universally attested
by early church leaders to be the same John Mark who was a
companion of Peter (1 Peter 5:13) and a cousin of Barnabas
(Colossians 4:10). At one point, he also accompanied Paul (Acts
12:25). Mark is purported to have recorded the recollections of
Peter near his death in Rome under Nero's persecution in the
mid-60s AD. Papias was reported by the early church historian
Eusebius as also saying: "Mark having become the interpreter of
Peter, wrote down accurately, though not in order, whatsoever he
remembered of the things said or done by Christ."[6]

Mark's authorship is further supported by several pieces of
internal evidence. For instance, the writing style suggests the
author spoke Aramaic, the common language in Israel. This
gospel also mentions Peter more frequently than the others,
including very near the beginning and at the end. And the perspective seems to be that of one of the twelve.[7] In particular, it
includes many vivid details that would only have been known to
Jesus' community, such as referring to "Alexander and Rufus"
(Mark15:21) being the sons of Simon of Cyrene. Equally
significant, the name Mark was attached to manuscripts dating
back to the second century. Mark was not a major figure in the
early church, so his name would not likely have been associated
with a Gospel unless he was the actual author. These facts fit

well with the traditional claim that the gospel is the recollections of Peter, recorded by Mark.

Matthew

Matthew was next to record a gospel included in the New Testament. It is commonly dated from the late 70s to the 80s, since its emphasis on Jesus' prophecies of the destruction of Jerusalem correspond to the memories of the Christians after the city was destroyed in AD 70. This dating range also fits the facts that it uses the gospel of Mark as one of its primary sources and that Matthew became a favorite gospel throughout the Christian world by the second century. The author is universally attributed by early church fathers to be the apostle Matthew. For instance, Iranaeus reports Papias as saying, "So then Matthew wrote the oracles in the Hebrew language, and every one interpreted them as he was able."[8]

The gospel of Matthew is actually written in Greek, but Matthew may have drawn on sayings of Jesus, which were passed on in Aramaic or Hebrew. Hence, Papias's reference to the Hebrew language. However, Greek was the preferred language for the final version of the Gospels since it was the common language of the region.

The authorship is further supported by internal evidence. In the story about a publican called to follow Jesus, the publican is called *Levi* in the gospels of Mark and Luke, but *Matthew* in Matthew. The author of Matthew would not likely have changed the name used in Mark unless it was his own. People at that time often used two names. In the same vein, Mark and Luke refer to "his house" (Mark 2:15; Luke 5:29); whereas, Matthew refers to "the house" (Matthew 9:10), as one would when writing of one's own house in a third-person narrative context. Matthew's writing also shows signs of Jewish religious training, and he has a strong command of Greek. These details fit well with the gospel's description of Matthew/Levi as a Levite and a tax collector.[9]

Luke

The author of the gospel of Luke is the physician who was one of Paul's traveling companions. Paul mentions him by name in several of his letters (Colossians 4:14; 2 Timothy 4:11; Philemon 24). Luke explicitly mentions himself as traveling with Paul during his later journeys in the "we" passages, which start in Acts 16:10. In addition, the authorship of Luke is uniformly supported by early church leaders. For instance, Irenaeus wrote, "Luke recorded the teachings of Paul after the deaths of Peter and Paul. He wrote after the Hebrew Matthew, at around the same time as Mark, and before John."[10] Irenaeus also records that Luke wrote Acts and traveled with Paul.[11] Luke's authorship is further confirmed by the early church leaders Clement,[12] Tertullian,[13] and Origen.[14]

Several pieces of internal evidence help to set the date for the writing of the gospel and the book of Acts in the 70s. For instance, Acts recounts in detail certain riots, which would have been counterproductive to reproduce unless they were still in people's memories and had to be addressed. The charge that Paul started riots would need to be explained during his custody and in the wake of his execution. In addition, Luke paraphrases Mark's end-time prophecies in such a way as to clearly connect them to the destruction of the temple in Jerusalem in AD 70. Reinforcing this association would have been important if the book was written when these traumatic events were fresh in the readers' minds. However, some scholars date Luke's writings even earlier, because these works end before Paul's death. Obviously, such a position would not weaken the argument for reliability but reinforce it even further.

John

The gospel of John is consistently testified by church tradition to have been written by the apostle John. For instance, Irenaeus in the second century quoted his contemporary acquaintance Polycarp, a pupil of the apostle John, as saying,

> John, the disciple of the Lord, who also had leaned upon His breast, did himself publish a Gospel during his residence at Ephesus in Asia . . . those who were conversant in Asia with John, the disciple of the Lord, [affirming] that John conveyed to them that information. And he remained among them up to the times of Trajan. . . . Then, again, the Church in Ephesus, founded by Paul, and having John remaining among them permanently until the times of Trajan, is a true witness of the tradition of the apostles.[15]

John also directly mentions himself as an eyewitness (John 19:35), and he implicitly refers to his presence as the disciple "whom Jesus loved" (13:23; 19:26; 20:2; 21:7; 21:20). Notably, the name John does not appear even though he is depicted in the other gospels as one of the three who are closest to Jesus. If John were the author, this notable absence would be understandable. And the perspective is from someone who was in the innermost circle. These facts also fit best with the traditional designation.

The gospel of John was written near the end of the first century. The date could not be later, since one of the oldest manuscript fragments discovered is a partial piece of the gospel of John. It is referred to as the John Ryland fragment, and it dates to the early second century.[16] The fragment was discovered in Egypt, so the gospel must have been written decades earlier to allow the needed time for a copy to migrate so far away from its original composition.

Why Are There Only Four Gospels?

The Gospels of the New Testament are the only ones accepted by early church leaders as part of the official collection of writings known as the New Testament canon. These canonical writings were chosen based on a very stringent set of criteria. First, the writers had to be eyewitnesses of Jesus or close associates of those who were. The writings also had to be recognized very early as authoritative in all regions of the Christian world. And they had to conform to the teaching that went directly back to the apostles. The Gospels meet these criteria. By the second century, the Gospels were recognized throughout the early church as uniquely authoritative. The church fathers quoted extensively from them. In fact, the entire New Testament could be reconstructed from their writings.

Other gospels also existed, such as the Gospel of Truth, Gospel of Mary, and Gospel of Peter. However, none of these noncanonical ones meet any of the previously mentioned criteria. They were typically composed more than a century after the New Testament was completed. They were not written by anyone even closely associated with the apostles, and they were not widely known. Their teaching also dramatically differed from that of the apostles. As such, their reliability and significance pale in comparison to the authentic four.

Despite these facts, one particular writing known as the Gospel of Thomas has gained greater popularity thanks to the extremely skeptical collection of New Testament scholars mentioned early in the book, known as the Jesus Seminar. They promoted Thomas alongside the canonical ones. Although their opinion did not represent the scholarly consensus, they did have the attention of the media. One of many of the members' main goals was to undermine trust of the New Testament, and they were successful in sowing the seeds of doubts in Christians who were not familiar with the actual evidence.

In truth, Thomas is simply a collection of sayings that were partially derived from the canonical gospels. None of its other content can be verified historically or archaeologically, and it was likely written in the mid second century. Most striking is that much of its teaching is completely at odds with everything we know about the historical Jesus. Despite the seminar's accolades, comparing the authentic Gospels to the Gospel of Thomas is much like comparing biographies of Abraham Lincoln written by distinguished Ivy League Lincoln scholars to the book *Abraham Lincoln: Vampire Hunter.*

Is What We Have Now, What They Wrote Then?

One of the stumbling blocks some skeptics face is that the Gospels were not copied from the original documents penned by the authors but from later copies (manuscripts). This concern is completely baseless, since virtually no other discovered historical documents are originals, unless they were chiseled in stone. The Gospels, like many ancient sources, were written on papyrus, which typically perished within a few hundred years. However, the extraordinary number of manuscripts, many of which are extremely early, ensure that we know the substance of what was originally written for the vast majority of gospel texts.

The Gospels are actually some of the highest-quality historical records from the ancient world. Leading scholar Dr. Dan Wallace describes the enormous amount of data for the New Testament as "an embarrassment of riches."[17] Most ancient biographies and histories were written well after the events they recorded. For instance, the earliest biography of Alexander the Great was written more than three centuries after the recorded events, and the information often came from third-hand accounts.[18] As such, we have better sources for the details of Jesus' life than for the details of Alexander's conquest of the known world. As a second example, all but one of the most valued written records for the emperor Tiberius Caesar, a contemporary of Jesus, were written eighty years, or later, after the described events.[19] In contrast, the four gospels were written between thirty and seventy years of Jesus' ministry. As such, we have more numerous and better sources for Jesus than for most famous ancient figures.

In addition, the number of copies of the original books of New Testament scriptures is vastly greater than for any other piece of ancient literature, totaling almost 5,800 Greek manuscripts. The next best example is the *Iliad* by Homer, which currently has roughly 1,800 discovered manuscripts. In addition, the earliest copies of New Testament scriptures are far closer to the originals. The time difference between the original copy of the *Iliad* and the first discovered copy is 350 to 400 years. Typically, the earliest copies of other ancient texts are more than 1,000 years later. In contrast, numerous copies of New Testament scriptures have been found dating within 300 years of their composition, and the earliest fragment is less than 50 years later.

The wealth and quality of the data has allowed New Testament scholars to accurately reconstruct the originals with an accuracy of 99 percent. Moreover, most of the remaining 1 percent of texts represent only spelling or other insignificant differences. The uncertainties that affect the actual meaning of passages amount to around 0.1 percent of the total. And none of these bring into question any major Christian doctrine or practice. Therefore, we can feel completely secure in knowing that the scriptures in our Bibles today are, for all practical purposes, the same as those penned by the original authors.[20]

The First Few Decades

As we discussed in the last chapter, historians agree that the gospel was proclaimed early, mere days after the tomb was found empty. The apostles' message centered on the belief that Jesus was the fulfillment of the Tanakh (the Old Testament Scriptures). The earliest New Testament books were written nineteen years after the resurrection. During the time before their writing, early Christians would have had the Old Testament Scriptures, their testimony of the resurrection, and the words of Jesus that the disciples remembered and orally passed on. I see a similar pattern in my own family. My kids can repeat the lines of our favorite movie, *Nacho Libre*, or my favorite, *It's a Wonderful Life*. They can also sing the words to scores of songs they have heard. Fortunately, the disciples lived in an oral culture, so they were much more skilled at remembering and accurately conveying information by word of mouth.[21] For instance, rabbis compiled and passed on the oral Torah to their disciples, who accurately transmitted the message from generation to generation. Jesus' disciples undoubtedly followed the same practice.

The reliability of the transmission of Jesus' life and teaching has been bolstered by studies in oral tradition in comparison to gospel texts. Most people in the first century could not read, so communities had developed effective tools to pass on stories orally. The teaching of Jesus matches these patterns. As New Testament scholar Mark D. Roberts comments:

> The oral forms of the Jesus tradition also ensured the truthful passing down of stories about him. Consider the example of the miracle stories in the Gospels. They almost always include the following elements: a statement of the problem; the brief description of the miracle; a statement of the response. This makes logical sense, of course, but it also conditions the mind to remember and relate miracle stories faithfully. It's rather like how jokes can take on a familiar form, thus helping us to remember them: "A priest, a minister, and a rabbi . . ." or "Knock, knock . . ."[22]

Jesus and His disciples structured their teaching in such a way as to ensure it was properly remembered and retaught. This type of oral tradition would not have become corrupted in the short interval between the events and the writing of the Gospels. So one does not even have to accept the traditional views of authorship to trust the Gospels' accuracy.

The Text Game

However, even stronger evidence supports our trust in the Gospels. I am sure you realize that your cell phone texts can still live on in the Cloud. In a court of law, they could be summoned and retrieved to compare what you say you said with what you actually wrote down in that text that you thought no one else would ever read. This example is a great way to see how the "text" of the Bible can be retrieved and compared as well.

Just as with texts, we can check the accuracy of the gospel writers by comparing them to each other and to Paul's writings. The Gospels clearly tell the same basic story since all of them overlap in numerous features, including the supernatural nature of Jesus' ministry; His basic teachings; the opposition He faced from the religious leaders; and His death, burial, and resurrection. The book of Acts also has numerous details in common with Paul's writings, including his visits to several cities, his floggings, and his discussions with the leaders in Jerusalem. In addition, Luke and Matthew both used Mark as a primary source, and they used a second common source often called Q. The significant similarities between parallel passages in Matthew and Luke (e.g., Matthew 3:7–10; Luke 3:7–9) and among the three gospels (Matthew 14:3–4; Mark 6:17–18; Luke 3:19–20) indicate that Luke and Matthew used their sources very accurately. The differences between the gospel accounts is no greater than the literary freedom that first-century biographers and historians typically employed.

Equally significant, the author of the gospel of Luke and of Acts explicitly states that his information came from eyewitnesses and other reliable records:

> Many have undertaken to draw up an account of the things that have been fulfilled among us, just as they were handed down to us by those who from the first were eyewitnesses and servants of the word. With this in mind, since I myself have carefully investigated everything from the beginning, I

too decided to write an orderly account for you, most excellent
Theophilus, so that you may know the certainty of the things
you have been taught. (Luke 1:1–4)

This introduction was typical for a first-century historical work that attempted to accurately describe the events. The
author mentions that many other written records were in existence, which he could likely access. In addition, he used sources
"by those who from the first were eyewitnesses and servants of
the word." In other words, he had access to the very eyewitnesses
of the actual events who became official leaders in the church.
These leaders undoubtedly ensured that Jesus' teachings and
ministry were accurately transmitted to the next generation. As
mentioned earlier, Luke even had access to Peter and James.

Embarrassing Testimony

Another category of evidence that supports the Gospels'
reliability is the inclusion of embarrassing testimony. Writers
would not make up events that intentionally made themselves
look bad. The Gospels are filled with this kind of evidence. For
instance, the disciples who would eventually become the leaders of the church are described in all of the gospel accounts as
abandoning or denying Jesus after He was arrested (e.g., Mark
14:50; Matthew 26:56; Luke 22:57; John 18:17). I have said in
countless settings on university campuses around the world, if
men were the sole authors of the Gospels, they would have made
themselves look a whole lot better. Mark Roberts concludes the
same thing in his book *Can We Trust the Gospels*: "If you read
through the four biblical Gospels, you'll find that the disciples
are almost never pictured as paragons of faith or wisdom. Time

and again they're portrayed negatively. This fact, all by itself, seems to me to disprove the power-grab thesis. If writers, editors, and collectors of the Gospels had been motivated by a desire for power, surely they would have cleaned up the Gospel record."[23]

Has Archaeology Confirmed the Narrative?

The reliability of the Gospels and Acts is further supported by archaeological evidence. Skeptical scholars had long claimed that many of the people, places, and other details mentioned in the Gospels were made up by the authors. However, a wealth of archaeological discoveries has overturned this belief. For instance, the remains were discovered for the cities of Bethlehem and Nazareth. And archaeologists discovered the remains of the synagogue in the city of Capernaum. Discoveries were also made of the coin with Caesar's image mentioned in Matthew 22:19 and the alabaster jar used to hold the perfume that anointed Jesus' feet (Mark 14:3). In addition, the pools of Siloam and Bethesda were also discovered to match the Gospels' descriptions.

Several other discoveries have confirmed the Gospels' descriptions of locations, topography, and people. Roberts comments:

The geography of the Gospels is clearly that of first-century Palestine, not some first-century Narnia. Once again, the evangelists put the major landmarks in the right places. When they place Capernaum by the Sea of Galilee, for example, this is correct. And when they refer to Jesus as going "up" to Jerusalem, even though he's traveling south, they get the elevation right, since a trip to Jerusalem involved going up, literally. The vast majority of geographical references in the

Gospels fit with what we know from other sources about the region in which Jesus ministered.[24]

The book of Acts has equally abundant details that have been verified, including names of leaders and their titles, local customs, and historical events. Such evidence has convinced many historical experts that Luke was one of the greatest historians of his time. The twentieth century's most renowned historian of Greco-Roman antiquity, Eduard Meyer, opined that Luke was a great historian and that Acts, "in spite of its more restricted content, bears the same character as those of the greatest historians, of a Polybius, a Livy, and many others."[25]

Any objective historian would conclude that the Gospels provide reliable accounts of Jesus' life and teaching. Those who challenge this view do not do so because of the evidence but in spite of it. They allow their biases against Christianity to blind them from the most sensible conclusion.

Despite all the compelling evidence, skeptics still attack the Gospels based on tensions between them. The next sections address their most common challenges. Their arguments, which at first seem formidable, will be shown to be little more than smoke and mirrors.

Contradictions or Variant Account?

When you listen to skeptics, they all have their favorite rants or sayings, much as you hear in political campaigns. They serve as rhetorical devices more than knockdown arguments against the faith. Bart Ehrman's favorite is when he reads a list of what he calls discrepancies in the Gospels and then consistently adds the phrase, *It depends on which gospel you read*. After reading off a dozen or so comparisons between similar incidents recorded in different gospels and highlighting the supposed conflict between the two accounts, he goes a long way in his own mind to convince his listeners that the evidence is overwhelming that the accounts are irreconcilable. He concludes that the testimony must, therefore, be dismissed in its entirety.[26] It is simply unreasonable to dismiss an event as historical because the eyewitness accounts appear to differ. A classic example is the sinking of the *Titanic*. Some eyewitnesses said the ship broke into two pieces before it sank, other eyewitnesses said it sunk in one piece. While the accounts may have differed, no one concludes that the *Titanic* didn't sink.[27]

When you look closer at the Gospels, many of these so-called discrepancies can be resolved when the distinction is made between a real contradiction and a variant account. For instance, when events are reported by journalists, there are a variety of ways the moment can be recounted without claiming these various stories are contradictory. If one report mentions only a specific person and the other refers to several, it simply means that the writers had different reasons for why they mentioned them. The same holds true for the Gospels (e.g., Matthew 20:30 versus Luke 18:35).

Ironically, the differences in the Gospels' accounts actually support their historical reliability. For they highlight the fact that the same story is being told by separate witnesses, so the overlapping details are almost certainly authentic. In fact, a detective named J. Warner Wallace carefully examined the gospel accounts as if he were examining the testimonies of witnesses in an investigation of a crime that had taken place decades in the past. He determined that the number of similarities and differences perfectly matched what would be expected if the basic story were true. In addition, the facts made no sense if the stories were fabricated. He started his investigation as an agnostic, but the evidence convinced him to become a Christian.[28]

As an example of one type of evidence, events in one gospel "interlock" with parallel descriptions in other gospels. For instance, Jesus asked Philip where they could buy food in John's account of a miraculous feeding (6:5), but no explanation is given as to why Philip was asked. In Luke we learn that this miracle occurred near Bethsaida (9:10), which was Philip's hometown (John 12:21). Jesus asking Philip, as described in John, makes sense with the additional information from Luke. These connections and other similar examples show that the gospel stories were based on actual historical events.[29]

Some details in the Gospels have not been fully reconciled with one another or with other historical sources. A classic example is specifics related to the census mentioned by Luke (2:1–3). However, no competent historian would ever reject the overall reliability of an ancient author based on a few tensions with other ancient documents, particularly when the author had been proven accurate in so many other details, such as with Luke. Moreover, apparent errors or inconsistencies in the Bible have consistently been vindicated upon further archaeological discoveries. Even with Luke's census, New Testament scholars have proposed plausible explanations of how every detail in the birth narrative is historically correct.[30] In summary, no tensions exist in the Gospels that in any relevant way undermine their trustworthiness.

Lost in Translation?

A second challenge is that many skeptics, and even Christians, expect the gospel authors to have written to their audiences as if they were writing to modern Westerners. However, it is an error to assume that the writing styles of the gospel writers are the same as those today. In other words, just as fashion is certainly different today than it was two thousand years ago, writing styles are also different. Can you imagine comparing clothing styles today to those of one hundred years ago? What about two thousand years ago? Judging the Gospels by the same standards as modern authors is like judging someone's style of dress one thousand years ago to today. This unrealistic rigidity in how students perceive the Bible has caused many to question their faith.

For instance, ancient historians were not necessarily concerned with chronology, and they would often paraphrase and summarize. This pattern explains many of the differences between parallel gospel accounts in exact wording, ordering of events, or other details. For instance, Mark mentions James and John asking Jesus to place them into a position of authority in His coming kingdom (Mark 10:35–37), while Matthew records their mother making the request (Matthew 20:20–21). This difference becomes easily understood in terms of the different original audiences. Matthew was writing to a Jewish community, so his audience would have understood that James and John were using their mother as an intermediary to make their request. The two authors wrote the event differently to their different audiences to best communicate the main point Jesus was making.

Some have seen such differences as serious challenges to the inspiration of the Bible, but this view is unfounded. God inspired the biblical authors to perfectly communicate His truth, but He did so using their own writing patterns and cultural contexts. In the same way that Jesus represents the incarnation of God in human form, the different books of the Bible represent God's divine truth incarnated into specific cultural and literary settings.

Another challenge relates to the issue of translation. Jesus spoke in Aramaic, but most of the gospel writers' audiences spoke Greek, which was like English today in terms of a global language. So Jesus' words had to be translated. When you translate statements from one language to another, it is important to convey the meaning of the sentence, not just the exact words. For instance, if I said in English, "The loss of the game really tore me up" and someone was translating that expression into Korean or Chinese, it might be conveyed in such a way that expresses my voice, not my exact words. It's always funny to me to say something in English that takes about fifteen seconds, and the translator talks about one minute in attempting to communicate my thought. I've heard lots of stories where something gets lost in translation or is paraphrased by the translator to get the point across.

In the same way, the New Testament writers had to translate Jesus' Aramaic teaching into Koine Greek, the common language of the time. Therefore, the Gospels record the Greek terms the Holy Spirit inspired the writers to choose that correspond to the Aramaic words Jesus spoke. "All Scripture is God-breathed and is useful for teaching, rebuking, correcting and training in righteousness" (2 Timothy 3:16).

SUMMARY

The weight of historical evidence demonstrates that the Gospels are very reliable. Many historians have come to recognize this fact, even if they did not originally accept that they were inspired and infallible. In fact, the Gospels stand head and shoulders above the vast majority of ancient literature in terms of manuscript evidence and support for historical accuracy.

When you are equipped with this knowledge, you can study Jesus' life and teachings with great confidence in their truth. Unlike the skeptics who think they can cobble together a picture of Jesus from unconnected historical events, you can see the clear vision of the Jesus of history and His mission to save the world. In the next few chapters we will see why the Gospels are more than reliable; they are the very word of God.

4

THE CRUCIFIXION

Why Jesus Had to Die

For the message of the cross is foolishness to
those who are perishing, but to us who are
being saved it is the power of God.

—1 Corinthians 1:18

THE RUSSIAN NOVELIST FYODOR DOSTOEVSKY WROTE his books during the turbulent nineteenth century, when the moral ground was dramatically shifting underneath his nation's feet. In one of his classics, *Crime and Punishment*, he explores the psychological torment of a young man who commits a double murder and tries to evade discovery of the crime as well as the mental and spiritual anguish that results. In the end he cannot escape from the accusations of his own conscience and turns himself in to the authorities. The message of this book, and other works, such as *The Brothers Karamazov*, is that there is a real moral code in the world that emanates from God from which we cannot escape. Therefore, there is a distinct moral principle that we all seem to accept: crime demands punishment.

For thousands of years of human history, the principle that someone committing a crime deserves just punishment has been widely accepted. Humans are innately moral beings with codes of conduct that demand retribution when violated. That desire is what we mean by *justice*. If someone is wronged, justice cries out that something be done. On the other hand, injustice is allowing evil actions to continue without any consequence to the perpetrators. Without punishment, injustice grows and flourishes.

What logically follows is that the *greater the crime, the more severe the punishment*. Some acts of violence are so serious that throughout civilization the ultimate punishment of death is enforced. Even societies against capital punishment assign such offenders life sentences. Taking away the rest of the criminal's life is seen as the only punishment that befits the crime.

These examples relate to crimes against humanity. But what about acts that go beyond what is done to other people? What about crimes against God? Would these acts not bring the greatest judgment of all since these are actually crimes of the heart against our Creator? The Ten Commandments begin with the ones that pertain to our relationship with God: we must have no other gods before Him; do not make idols and worship them; do not take the name of the Lord in vain; and remember His Sabbath (Exodus 20:1–11). After these come the commandments that speak of our relationship with one another as people. But the perplexing question is, how are our sins against God to be treated?

The God of love is also a God of judgment. The reason? If He does not judge sin, He could not ultimately be loving. Imagine your parents not stopping your sibling from assaulting you because they told you they were loving parents. If they were truly loving, they would stop the offending party and punish him for his actions. The punishment acts as a deterrent against committing the offense again. People indeed want God to stop evil, but the way He does it is through judgment.

Yes, people have "free will," but so does God. People can act as they choose, but God will ultimately respond. Ironically, when God is recorded as judging evil people, critics accuse Him of being harsh and unloving. However, God only punishes people and nations out of love for the entire world, and His judgments, even the most severe, are always just. Unfortunately, everyone has violated God's law and acted in ways that hurt others and undermined His creation. Therefore, we all deserve judgment, even death. So then the quandary is this: How can God be both loving and just at the same time without compromising either?

The answer to this question is connected to His death on the cross, which, as we discussed in chapter 2, is an accepted fact of history. In essence, Jesus died on the cross to suffer the consequences for the sins of humankind (fulfilling the demands of justice) while extending mercy to us, who deserved the punishment. Christ came in fulfillment of the prophets to suffer and die. He freely gave his life for ours (John 10:15) so we would be free from the power and judgment of sin. Though the cross has become the universally recognized symbol of the Christian faith, its power has been obscured and its horror vastly understated.

God isn't just interested in the evil that happens *to you*; He wants to stop it coming *through you*.

WHY CRUCIFIXION?

God chose the specific moment in history for this death to happen at the hands of those who were infamous for being the best, most efficient, cruelest, and most unrelenting in their ability to kill someone in such a fashion that it could never be credibly doubted.

It was public. To have Jesus die in some kind of private, humane way would have meant that the world could be left to doubt whether He really died or think that His followers staged an apparent execution, much like a team working with an illusionist. The actual form of execution placed a crater in the heart of human history.

The medical details of the crucifixion have been studied extensively based on the gospel accounts, historical evidence, and Jesus' burial cloth. As depicted in the Gospels, those condemned to crucifixion were first flogged using a whip consisting of leather straps with pieces of metal and bone attached to them. This scourging would deeply rip into the flesh of the victim, causing extensive bleeding. Jesus also had a crown of thorns pressed onto His head, causing even more blood loss. The victim would then carry the crossbeam of the cross, which weighed around one hundred pounds, to the site of the crucifixion. At that point, the wrists[1] and feet would be nailed to the cross. The nails were the size of railroad spikes, and they severed a major nerve, which caused excruciating pain. After the soldiers placed the victim on the cross, they would commonly jeer and divide up the clothes. These details are mentioned in the Gospels, and they precisely match the specifics of Roman crucifixions. Such correspondences further confirm that the authors were recording actual events derived from eyewitnesses.

The posture of crucified individuals prevented breathing, so they had to pull themselves up by their arms and feet to breathe. Victims would commonly cease to breathe due to exhaustion or pain and then die from lack of oxygen. Others would die from dehydration or blood loss. If the soldiers wished to speed up the death, they would break the legs, as mentioned in the gospel of John. Jesus appeared to already be dead, so they drove a spear through His side to make sure. Roman soldiers always ensured that their victims had truly died before allowing them to be taken off the cross, or else they themselves would be executed.[2]

Just knowing that Jesus died is not enough; one must understand the significance of His death. Thousands of people die every day. We don't think that their deaths have any effect on us, other than the sadness of the loss of someone we knew or loved. But the death of Jesus has everything to do with us. The knowledge of His crucifixion isn't about eliciting emotion or sadness on our part but a conviction of what was accomplished on our behalf. His mission to save us was what drove Him beyond the pain and torment. "Looking unto Jesus, the author and finisher of our faith, who for the joy set before Him endured the cross, despising the shame, and has sat down at the right hand of the throne of God" (Hebrews 12:2 NKJV).

This inexplicable joy is the secret of how Jesus endured that moment. It was the joy of knowing what His sacrifice would accomplish for all humanity. We now turn our attention to understanding the greatness of what was accomplished through His death on the cross—starting with His satisfaction of the claims of guilt against us because of our transgressions.

GOD'S PLAN TO END INJUSTICE

As we look deeply into this supreme act of divine justice, we should shudder at its implications for us and our salvation. God initially created the world free of evil and suffering. The first couple existed in a perfect relationship with God, each other, and creation. They only needed to trust God as the source of their identity, security, and purpose. However, Adam and Eve chose to rebel against God and become their own ultimate authority. Their rebellion resulted in their separation from God, the source of true life. They then experienced pain and suffering, which spread to the entire world. Yet God did not abandon humanity. Instead, He set in motion His plan of salvation to save us from both the consequences of sin and its destructive power.

The plan of salvation started with the first sacrifice—the death of an animal in the garden to create a covering for Adam and Eve's sin. It extended to the formation of the nation of Israel with their sacrificial system, which covered the sins of the Hebrew people. It culminated in the sacrifice of Jesus on the cross for the sins of the whole world. And it will be fully enacted with Jesus' second coming, when all evil will be removed and people fully experience God's presence forever in the restored creation.

To digress for just a moment, critics balk at the notion that Adam and Eve were real people, but several factors point to their authenticity. From science, the fossil record suggests that the characteristics distinct in humans appeared suddenly and did not evolve gradually over time.[3] In addition, genetic evidence is consistent with all people originating from a single couple.[4] Next, Jesus spoke about God creating male and female in the beginning (Matthew 19:4). As we have mentioned, and will discuss in greater detail in the next chapter, the resurrection of Jesus validates His identity and gives credibility to His words above all others. If Jesus said Adam and Eve were real, then you can confidently accept that claim as truth. Finally, no theological premise is more empirically supported than the fallen condition of humankind. People have an innate sense that absolute moral principles exist, yet we have an uncontrollable tendency to violate those truths, often through the most horrendous acts.[5] These realities are abundantly confirmed by even the most cursory study of history, psychology, or the evening news. And they point to the fact that we were created by God in His image, but humanity became corrupt and alienated from our Creator.

The Penalty of Sin

The first issue Christ had to deal with was the penalty for sin. Because sin is, in essence, breaking God's law through rebelling against Him, it must be punished. Imagine a murderer committing a horrible crime and simply asking to be forgiven and let out of jail. Forgiveness can be granted, but what's missing is a just punishment.

The physical and emotional trauma of what Christ suffered and endured is difficult to comprehend even when graphically portrayed in movies like *The Passion of the Christ*. Usually, the response is that this torture and pain was for the purpose of Jesus showing us how much He loves us. This claim is true for a different reason than most assume. Yes, it was done out of incomprehensible love. But just as important, He took our punishment. It was the penalty for the sins of the world. Whether we realize it or not, this punishment was ours to bear. It is astounding that someone would bear these consequences on our behalf.

The prophet Isaiah would predict this substitutionary work of Jesus on the cross, how He took our punishment and paid the penalty for the sins of the world:

> We all, like sheep, have gone astray,
>> each of us has turned to our own way;
> and the LORD has laid on him
>> the iniquity of us all. (Isaiah 53:6)

This graphic prophetic picture was given almost six hundred years in advance, and it depicts the demands of divine justice as portrayed throughout Scripture.

From the beginning of God's dealings with humans, sin (breaking God's law) was costly. However, God constantly provided coverings and substitutes. The first act of disobedience resulted in death's entering into the human condition. Immediately, an innocent animal was killed to cover the first couple's transgression and consequent shame. The deliverance from the bondage of slavery in Egypt was punctuated with the Hebrews being given a shelter from the judgment coming to the land by the blood of a lamb. The promise of God was that the blood would cause the judgment of the final plague to pass over the dwellings of those who applied it to their doorposts. Hence, the term *Passover*. Through the sacrifice of the lamb, the Hebrews were spared from the death of their firstborn.

This theme of the price of sin being the shedding of blood is consistent through Scripture. Jesus would point to this symbolically in His last supper with His disciples before His death. He would raise the wine glass used in the Passover seder and declare,

"This cup is the new covenant in my blood, which is poured out for you" (Luke 22:20).

Understanding the gravity of sin and the extreme penalty that is incurred should make us tremble at the enormity of this great sacrifice and gift from God that He would suffer such torment and agony in our place.

Severe Punishment Overshadowed by Great Mercy

What is often overlooked when the severe punishments for sin in the Old Testament are mentioned is the enormous mercy that is available to all. Put simply, when you realize the gravity of the consequences of a transgression, you will be amazed at the grace that is offered. On the other hand, if the penalty for sin were negligible, then the value of forgiveness would also be diminished.

The prime example of God's provision for sin is seen in the book of Leviticus. This part of Scripture is often attacked by critics as a prime exhibit where God's wrath is too excessive. However, a closer look reveals the opposite. Before Leviticus mentions laws and punishments, the first sixteen of twenty-seven chapters provide instructions for atonement (covering for sins) and for receiving forgiveness and cleansing. In chapter 16 the instructions for the Day of Atonement demonstrate a grand picture of how abundant and available God's mercy has always been.

This day of forgiveness is still observed thirty-five hundred years later. Once a year, the Day of Atonement, "Yom Kippur" in Hebrew, is celebrated around the world. Virtually every Jewish synagogue reads the book of Jonah during the ceremony. This choice of reading may seem odd at first glance. Why would the book where the key story is about a man being swallowed by a sea creature rise to such attention? The choice is not simply a peculiarity of the Jewish faith. Looking closer, it's not the fish story that is the biggest surprise of this account but the gift of mercy that swallows up the judgment that the city of Nineveh was due.

In the story, Jonah runs away after God sends him to deliver a message of destruction to the city. Many assume that Jonah ran because he was afraid to deliver this stern warning to such a hostile city. But the real reason Jonah ran was because he knew God was merciful. In the end, he told God that he didn't want to give the message of judgment to the people, for he knew God would forgive and not destroy them.

> But to Jonah this seemed very wrong, and he became angry. He prayed to the LORD, "Isn't this what I said, LORD, when I was still at home? That is what I tried to forestall by fleeing to Tarshish. I knew that you are a gracious and compassionate God, slow to anger and abounding in love, a God who relents from sending calamity. Now, LORD, take away my life, for it is better for me to die than to live." (Jonah 4:1–3)

Many times we as humans want people to get what they deserve. When Jonah was told to announce impending doom on the city, he was only too aware of God's great mercy—so much so that he ran as far away from it as he could. Thankfully, you can't outrun the love of God. "But God demonstrates his own love for us in this: While we were still sinners, Christ died for us" (Romans 5:8).

The Lamb of God

God demonstrated His love and abundant mercy through many other Old Testament characters in addition to Jonah. But these figures were merely foreshadowing the fulfillment of God's promises in the entrance of Jesus of Nazareth into human history. His coming was later heralded by John the Baptist, one of the key people that even critics concede was a person of history. John preached repentance for the forgiveness of sins in the wilderness of Judea, and he baptized multitudes who responded. Seeing Jesus at a distance he announced "Behold! The Lamb of God who takes away the sins of the world" (John 1:29 NKJV).

Calling Him the Lamb of God harkened to the images of the sacrificial lamb that averted judgment for all who took advantage of this offer of grace. It also foreshadowed that Jesus would sacrifice His unblemished life to remove the sins of the world. Jesus recognized that His sacrifice was the culmination of His earthly mission. "I am the living bread that came down from heaven. Whoever eats this bread will live forever. This bread is my flesh, which I will give for the life of the world" (John 6:51). Again the ultimate price of sin points to the shedding of blood as the required payment.

Lifted Up

The apostle John in his gospel detailed another moment of divine judgment upstaged by God's mercy. The setting was a plague that broke out among the Hebrews while they were in the wilderness following their miraculous deliverance from Egypt. In one of the strangest moments in history, God instructed Moses on what to do to stop the plague:

And the people spoke against God and against Moses: "Why have you brought us up out of Egypt to die in the wilderness? For there is no food and no water, and our soul loathes this worthless bread." So the LORD sent fiery serpents among the people, and they bit the people, and many of the people of Israel died.

Therefore the people came to Moses, and said, "We have sinned, for we have spoken against the LORD and against you; pray to the LORD that He take away the serpents from us." So Moses prayed for the people.

Then the LORD said to Moses, "Make a fiery serpent, and set it on a pole, and it shall be that everyone who is bitten, when he looks at it, shall live." So Moses made a bronze serpent, and put it on a pole; and so it was, if a serpent had bitten anyone, when he would looked at the bronze serpent, he lived. (Numbers 21:5–9 NKJV)

This indeed is one of those strange moments in history where we shouldn't dismiss the message because of the unique and unusual nature of the narrative. The story can be summarized by the common pattern seen throughout the Old Testament: sin brought judgment, but God then provided mercy.

The remedy God prescribed was to make a symbol of the people's judgment and lift it up to the place where everyone had a chance to look at it and be forgiven. They were instructed to look and live. One could imagine the difficulty of the people looking to God's solution with all the turmoil around them. When I'm in a place of panic and fear, getting my eyes off my problem and looking to God's solution takes a great step of faith.

Jesus would use this imagery to describe His mission. "And

as Moses lifted up the serpent in the wilderness, even so must the Son of Man be lifted up, that whoever believes in him should not perish but have eternal life. For God so loved the world that He gave his only begotten Son, that whoever believes in him should not perish but have everlasting life" (John 3:14–16 NKJV).

Jesus promised that people should look to Him when He was lifted up on the cross to receive eternal life. As with the serpents, His sacrifice represented the judgment deserved for our sins. And placing our faith in Him would result in our being freed from the curse of death. The apostle Paul would give more insight into this when he wrote "God made him who had no sin to be sin for us, so that in him we might become the righteousness of God" (2 Corinthians 5:21).

The reason a serpent was used is possibly connected to the moment that Jesus took on our sins at the cross. The verse mentioned above said he became "sin for us, who knew no sin" (KJV). As the apostle Peter stated, "He himself bore our sins in his body on the cross, so that we might die to sins and live for righteousness; by his wounds you have been healed" (1 Peter 2:24).

Once again the prophet Isaiah spoke of this bearing of our sins hundreds of years in advance:

> Surely he took up our pain
> and bore our suffering,
> yet we considered him punished by God,
> stricken by him, and afflicted.
> But he was pierced for our transgressions,
> he was crushed for our iniquities;
> the punishment that brought us peace was on him,
> and by his wounds we are healed. (Isaiah 53:4–5)

This dimension of salvation was not what the Jewish people were expecting when they looked for a Messiah. They had hoped for a national, militaristic deliverance, not the spiritual salvation that was desperately needed. The idea of their Messiah being tortured and humiliated was scandalous to them. Yet this incredible sacrifice made real peace with God possible.

Redeemed from Slavery

Jesus also came to deal with sin's power over us. The announcement of Christ's birth by an angel was accompanied by this prophecy: "He will save his people from their sins" (Matthew 1:21). The incredible gift to us isn't just forgiveness but the power to overcome our inborn proclivity toward evil. The Old Testament prophets promised that God would give His people a new heart (Ezekiel 36:26; Jeremiah 31:31–33). This promise was fulfilled by the Holy Spirit giving believers a new nature—a new spiritual birth. The process of God freeing us from the power of sin is connected by the New Testament writers to God's freeing the Hebrews from the slavery of Egypt.

Many of the issues that skeptics point to in order to discredit the Scriptures actually point to the mercy and love of God when examined openly and fairly. Slavery is certainly one of humanity's greatest transgressions. From the beginning of recorded history, slavery in one form or another has been a fact of life. People have claimed that the Bible somehow sanctioned slavery because there were instructions given about how slaves were to be treated. Though this is not the place to give a full exposé about how to properly interpret this issue and how fair and just God was to those who were in this condition, it is important to see that slavery was the picture God gave that best described the human condition.[6] We are slaves to sin.

The Ten Commandments, which God personally gave to Moses, begin with the statement, "I am the LORD your God, who brought you out of Egypt, out of the land of slavery" (Exodus 20:2). Then the commandments are listed. God is not the author of slavery but the deliverer from it.

It is impossible to understand what Christ accomplished through His crucifixion without grasping the fact that He came to buy us out of this condition of spiritual bondage. That's what the term *redeemed* means—to buy or ransom someone from a condition of slavery and set that person free. "For even the Son of Man did not come to be served, but to serve, and to give his life as a ransom for many" (Mark 10:45). To be ransomed suggests we were held hostage in our fallen condition. The prophets would foretell this redemption, and Christ would fulfill it through His death and resurrection.

The Crucifixion Is at the Heart of the Gospel

We are called to proclaim the gospel (good news) to all nations. To gain a better understanding of what the message is, here is a succinct definition:

> The **gospel** is the good news that God became man in Jesus Christ. He lived the life we should have lived and died the death we should have died—in our place. Three days later He rose from the dead, proving that He is the Son of God and offering the gift of salvation to those who repent and believe in Him.

At the heart of the message is the sentence, "He lived the life we should have lived and died the death we should have died—in our place." Let's look closer at each idea presented. (In the next few chapters we examine the other claims of the gospel message.)

He Lived the Life We Should Have Lived

Christ had to be spotless. He wasn't just an extraordinarily righteous man; He was perfect. In all of human history there has been no serious claim to being perfect, especially in the moral sense. British comedian Stephen Fry unleashed a grossly unfair rant against God due to the evil and suffering in the world and laid it all out in his charge that God couldn't be real and allow such pain. He went on to say that he would like it better if the Greek gods were real because they were more like humans, with the same appetites and moral imperfections. Is this really what we would want—an imperfect God?

After proving again and again His avoidance of sin, Jesus' final test would be to surrender Himself to God and be willing to do His will, even if it meant death. Throughout the ministry of Jesus, He gave a variety of messages that pointed to His primary mission to lay down His life for others. Quite the antithesis of the survival-of-the-fittest mentality. It was a revolutionary outlook that would be the radical call for His followers. If He did not come to be served but to serve others, then this would be His followers' path as well, a radical love of action, not just talk. Self-sacrifice would replace self-fulfillment as the path to peace and life.

Because of His sinless life, He was able to offer Himself on our behalf as our substitute. The only appropriate sacrifice to cover the sins of the entire world was a perfect one. Only Jesus could fulfill this requirement. He was not just an extraordinarily righteous man; He was completely free from sin and perfectly obedient to God in all His words and deeds. All of our heroes are flawed, even the best of them. However, Jesus completely followed God's law and His will. He demonstrated unparalleled compassion and mercy. He also displayed complete authority over evil powers, disease, and even death itself. He challenged religious hypocrisy, and He called people to completely turn from evil. In the end, He fully surrendered Himself to God's will by offering Himself as a sacrifice on the cross. Jesus' life fulfilled God's law, so His death was able to cover all of our sins.

In addition, through our faith in Jesus, the power of the Holy Spirit unites our lives with His. So we become transformed daily into His image. Over time we experience greater power over our sins, and our very thoughts to greater and greater extent conform to God's will. We can also experience peace and joy, knowing that God does not see us in the light of our own imperfections but in the light of Jesus' life.

He Died the Death We Should Have Died

The idea of dying for someone else's sin seems senseless to many. The Muslim world rejects this concept and states that each person will be judged for his or her own actions. Most religious systems state that our eternal fate is determined by how well our actions conform to some moral code or set of teachings. Unfortunately, all such claims are foolish when we recognize that no one can meet God's perfect standards. As the apostle Paul stated, "All . . . fall short of the glory of God" (Romans 3:23).

Everyone who commits a crime against humanity should pay for that crime. But how could one pay for his sins against

God? What possible punishment would fit rebellion against the Creator of the universe? If certain acts merit death or a life sentence here on earth, wouldn't it make sense for the punishment for sins against God to be even greater? Would not the consequences of sins against an eternal God also continue on into eternity? The sobering truth is that all of us deserve the judgment of eternal death since no one is worthy to stand in God's presence. Only in this light can the sacrifice of Jesus be properly understood. All of us deserve punishment, but Jesus' perfect life paid the unimaginable debt we owe God. Through faith in Him, we receive forgiveness of our sins and the power to live a new life. As the apostle Paul wrote to the Romans:

> This righteousness is given through faith in Jesus Christ to all who believe. There is no difference between Jew and Gentile, for all have sinned and fall short of the glory of God, and all are justified freely by his grace through the redemption that came by Christ Jesus. God presented Christ as a sacrifice of atonement, through the shedding of his blood—to be received by faith. He did this to demonstrate his righteousness, because in his forbearance he had left the sins committed beforehand unpunished—he did it to demonstrate his righteousness at the present time, so as to be just and the one who justifies those who have faith in Jesus. (Romans 3:22–26)

It indeed was a divine rescue mission. Christ came to ransom us from the grip of sin and death. Yet it must be underscored: there was no other way to help us except through His substitutionary death on our behalf. If there had been another way other than dying in our place, Jesus would have certainly taken that way out. In fact, before His death He prayed in the Garden of Gethsemane, "If there be any other way, let this cup pass." In the end, there was no other way. The sinless Son of God offered Himself to the Father on our behalf to pay for our sins and bring us back to God.

THE IMPACT OF THE CROSS OF CHRIST

Christ's crucifixion is undeniable. However, beyond the fact of His death, the significance of what happened is found as we look deeper into Scripture. To some it seems like a brutal, tragic end to a great life. In reality, there were far-reaching consequences to this sacrificial act—as far-reaching as to heaven above and hell below.

Disarmed the Powers of Darkness

The evil powers of this world had conspired to destroy Jesus. These powers included the corrupt religious system headed by Caiaphas, the domineering political system headed by Pilate and Herod Antipas, and the demonic powers ruled by Satan. Their ultimate victory seemed to be Jesus' crucifixion, but He would soon demonstrate His victory over their power at the resurrection. Moreover, by paying for our sins, He took their power over the world away from them:

> When you were dead in your sins and in the uncircumcision of your flesh, God made you alive with Christ. He forgave us all our sins, having canceled the charge of our legal indebtedness, which stood against us and condemned us; he has taken it

away, nailing it to the cross. And having disarmed the powers and authorities, he made a public spectacle of them, triumphing over them by the cross." (Colossians 2:13–15)

As a result, we now have authority over the evil spiritual powers of this world. As such, we can break spiritual strongholds oppressing our lives and those of other believers. We can also pray for God's authority and power to break through the oppression covering local communities, cities, and nations. This dramatic change made possible by His death cannot be overstated.

Delivered Us from the Fear of Death

Since the children have flesh and blood, he too shared in their humanity so that by his death he might break the power of him who holds the power of death—that is, the devil—and free those who all their lives were held in slavery by their fear of death.

—Hebrews 2:14–15

The most sobering fact of life is that everyone dies. The knowledge of this can cause some to become so absorbed in the business and the affairs of life that they simply distract themselves from thinking about this ominous fate. Others live in a silent desperation because of the prospect of this unavoidable end. Great philosophers grappled with this and wrote about dealing with the existential despair of a life that begins for no reason and ends with no real meaning. However, because of His death, we have been set free from this pit of hopelessness. No longer are we held prisoner by the fear of death. We know that there is something beyond this life.

Broke Down the Wall of Division

But now in Christ Jesus you who formerly were far off have been brought near by the blood of Christ. For He Himself is our peace, who made both groups into one and broke down the barrier of the dividing wall, by abolishing in His flesh the enmity, which is the Law of commandments contained in ordinances, so that in Himself He might make the two into one new man, thus establishing peace, and might reconcile them both in one body to God through the cross, by it having put to death the enmity.

—Ephesians 2:13–16 NASB

There was no greater ethnic divide than that between Jew and Gentile. The Scripture says that because of His death that wall was torn down through being united in Christ. Our world today continues to be divided and torn because of the evil of racism. This stems from the darkness that resides in every human heart. We look negatively on other groups of people due to our own fear, insecurities, and harsh judgments. Many cannot forgive the sins committed by a few members of some group, so they look at everyone in that group through the lens of their stereotypes. Or they simply show no concern for the hardships of those outside of their communities. Only the power of the cross can break through many of these barriers. God forgiving us of our many sins motivates us to forgive others. And God's mercy and kindness toward us compels us to the show the same to even our enemies.

Turning to Jesus results in God's adopting us as His children. Our identities no longer rest in our ethnicities, socio-economic status, or any other natural criteria. We recognize that we now belong to a new family, which crosses all natural divisions. Paul vividly described this reality in relation to the division that had previously existed between the Jewish people and Gentiles (non-Jews). During the time of Moses, God instituted laws to create cultural barriers between His people and the surrounding nations, such as not eating together. The purpose was to prevent the idolatry and corruption of the surrounding nations from polluting Israel. After Jesus, the Holy Spirit would empower believers to live righteously even in the midst of the pagan culture. The barriers were no longer needed, so both Jews and Gentiles could come together as one people. The same uniting power exists today, which can bring together all people.

One of the most powerful pictures of this unity was on the day of Pentecost (Acts 2). During this festival, Jewish people from all parts of the world came together in Jerusalem. One day after the disciples had been praying, the Holy Spirit fell on them, and they started to speak in the different languages of the visitors. Everyone heard the wonders of God in his own language. This unifying event undid the curse of the tower of Babel (Genesis 11:1–9), where God separated the people of the world into different languages to prevent the destructive power of the unity that was born in their rebellion.

SUMMARY

On September 11, 2001, Islamic terrorists flew hijacked airliners into the World Trade Center towers in New York. The devastation brought America to its knees. The site of the attack become known as Ground Zero, a name that continues to be used today.

During the days and weeks following the attacks, the rescue workers erected a cross, made from the twisted steel taken out of the rubble of the fallen towers. The pain and suffering of the cross was an immediate reminder that God is well acquainted with our grief and our sorrows. It was also a reminder that even in the midst of tragedy, there can be hope for tomorrow.

Today millions come to New York to visit the memorial at Ground Zero. They come perhaps to remember loved ones or friends that were lost on that fateful day. Others come in search of answers to the reasons why such bizarre, cruel events take place. In the end, the hope is that healing and peace can somehow be found from that visit to this hallowed piece of history.

In a way, the cross of Christ represents the ultimate Ground Zero in human history. At the cross the greatest injustice in history took place. Jesus Christ, the only perfect person who had ever lived, suffered and died for the sins of others. Regardless of our age, ethnicity, or religious background, when we visit *that* Ground Zero and remember the ultimate sacrifice that was made on our behalf, it gives us the hope we need in the midst of the confusing and dark times we live in, as well as the power that lifts us into real grace and a lasting peace that passes all understanding.

5

THE RESURRECTION

The Event that Changed Everything

*The evidence for the resurrection is better than
for claimed miracles in any other religion. It's
outstandingly different in quality and quantity.*[1]
—ANTONY FLEW, FAMED ATHEIST TURNED BELIEVER IN GOD

A PHILOSOPHER OF SCIENCE, KARL POPPER, PRO-
posed a definitive way to determine whether something could be
considered scientifically credible. Rather than trying to establish
conclusively what is true, he instead proposed that the key test
was whether something could be proven false.[2] This standard
of testing has become a part of the scientific and philosophical
vocabulary and has been deemed a corollary of the scientific
method that is universally acknowledged.

In light of the vast ocean of information that surrounds us,
where verifying the credibility of claims or verification of identity
is vital, we must have a set of rules to help eliminate the false and
fraudulent. Such criteria help to expose posers and imposters. In

addition, we must remember that the existence of counterfeits does not mean that something real does not exist.

Some assume that religious or metaphysical claims are automatically eliminated based on Popper's criterion. The typical retort is that religious claims cannot be verified. Therefore, they should stay out of any discussion that is attempting to discover the answer to ultimate questions. Many are shocked to realize that not all religious claims are excluded when this restriction is applied.

What stands out is the unequivocal distinction of the Christian faith. It is the only religion whose central tenet of faith is able to be tested in this manner. That claim is that Jesus Christ was bodily resurrected three days after His crucifixion. This was the primary message of His disciples that turned the world upside down. The apostle Paul would write to the Corinthians: "If Christ has not been raised . . . your faith is in vain" (1 Corinthians 15:14 ESV).

Let me say it again as clearly and succinctly as possible. Christianity stands or falls on a singular event: the resurrection of Jesus Christ from the dead. It not only is the foundation for a credible faith, but it is a realistic hope from the suffocating uncertainty of what lies beyond the grave.

Other religions, such as Islam, offer subjective tests to validate their claims. For instance, the Koran states that the reader should ask if anyone could write a book like the Koran (Sura 10:37–38). But how could such a claim be disproven? After all, one could just as easily ask if anyone could write a book like the *Iliad* or *Moby Dick*?

Hinduism makes no attempt to verify itself. The stories about the gods are simply told and the weight of centuries of cultural momentum carry it forward. In other words, if the stories are told long enough, they become a part of the cultural narrative. There is no evangelistic mandate to send Hindu missionaries with any kind of message for others to believe. If there are millions of gods, as they believe, then convincing people to add one more would be needless.

Buddhism doesn't depend on whether Buddha was a real person and certainly not on a claim on his part or his followers that he was God or a representative of God. Buddhism at its core requires an adherence to a set of philosophical commitments to right thinking and right living. As William Lane Craig and Sean McDowell comment:

> Buddha reportedly said, "By this you shall know that a man is not my disciple that he tries to work a miracle" (Huston Smith, *The World's Religions*, 1991, p. 97). Jesus said and did just the exact opposite! Jesus did miracles so that people would *know* he was God's Son (e.g., Mark 2:1–10). Unlike Buddha, Jesus gave evidence so people would have a confident faith in him.[3]

But the message of Jesus Christ is for all peoples and all nations. One of the many distinctions was that no command existed to export a specific culture (such as Jewish culture). Instead, the commission was given to spread the message that Jesus had been raised from the dead to all peoples and to allow His Spirit to guide them. God is not interested in eliminating the culture of any nation. He is interested in transforming hearts and minds. When this happens, the culture will experience a rebirth of its best parts and purposes. The distinctive of every people group and ethnicity point to the diversity and creativity of God in creating such a wide variety of people. As the apostle Paul would say, "He has made from one blood every nation of men to dwell on all the face of the earth . . . so that they should seek the Lord" (Acts 17:26–27 NKJV).

THE BEST EXPLANATION OF
THE MINIMAL FACTS

In chapter 2, we examined the minimal facts surrounding the death of Jesus accepted by most scholars, even skeptical ones. Again, these are facts that even skeptical scholars accept as true. Let's quickly review the primary ones:

- Jesus was crucified by Pontius Pilate, the Roman governor.
- Three days later the tomb was found empty by a few of His female followers.
- His disciples believed Jesus appeared to them following His death.
- The message of His resurrection was proclaimed immediately after this reappearance to the disciples.
- Saul of Tarsus, the chief persecutor of His followers, became a believer.

Because these facts are accepted as part of the historical bedrock, we can use them to demonstrate that the only plausible explanation for the events at the end of His ministry is that Jesus actually rose from the dead. N. T. Wright, one of the foremost experts on the resurrection, agreed that an actual resurrection was the best explanation of the facts. "The only possible reason why early Christianity began and took the shape it did is that the tomb really was empty and that people really did meet Jesus, alive again, and . . . though admitting it involves accepting a challenge at the level of worldview itself, the best historical explanation for all these phenomena is that Jesus was indeed bodily raised from the dead."[4]

The implications of even skeptics accepting the minimal facts cannot be overstated. For decades, radical skeptics have tried to suggest that there was very little we could know outside the New Testament about Jesus. Understanding how erroneous this claim is gives a glimpse into the desperate efforts to dismiss the real historical evidence for Jesus Christ. On top of that, we have seen how equally dismissive they have been about the Gospels and the rest of the New Testament. These are reliable historical documents as well and should be included in the quest for the historical Jesus. The reality is that skeptics indeed use the New Testament, cherry-picking what they like and throwing out what they don't like based on presuppositions and biases, as we discussed in chapter 3. However, anyone who examines the evidence fairly will inevitably come to the conclusion that the resurrection happened.

As theologian Wolfhart Pannenberg said, "As long as historiography does not begin dogmatically with a narrow concept of reality according to which 'dead men do not rise,' it is not clear why historiography should not in principle be able to speak about Jesus' resurrection as the explanation that is best established of such events as the disciples' experiences of the appearances and the discovery of the empty tomb."[5]

THE FAILURE OF NATURALISTIC THEORIES

Based on the minimal facts, one might naturally ask if Christians have proven the resurrection. The answer depends on what one assumes the meaning of *proven* to be and on what one believes is possible. For the Christian, the evidence points unequivocally to Jesus' having been raised from the dead. However, skeptics assume from the beginning that all supernatural claims are false, for nothing exists outside of nature. As such, people simply do not rise from the dead. Therefore, any explanation in their minds, no matter how seemingly improbable, is preferable to believing the resurrection actually happened.

The most popular skeptical alternative today is the hallucination theory. It acknowledges that the disciples believed that they encountered the risen Jesus, but their experience was simply a hallucination driven by grief and disillusionment. This theory is primarily promoted by nonmedical writers without any real knowledge of the subject. Competent medical professionals have pointed out that such vivid hallucinations would never take place in groups or with so many individuals at different times (e.g., Paul and James) in different locations. In addition, such vivid hallucinations would have required the disciples to have expected the appearances. Yet the disciples clearly had no such expectation since they fled the scene. Other witnesses, such as James the brother of Jesus, were in a completely normal state of mind, so nothing would have produced any sort of vision or perceived encounter. Nor would this theory account for the empty tomb. As physician Joseph W. Bergeron and Habermas wrote, "In sum, psychiatric hypotheses offer no acceptable explanations for the individual or simultaneous group encounters of the disciples with the resurrected Jesus."[6]

Another common theory is that the resurrection claims are primarily legends, made up decades after the events. This theory requires virtually all of the key historical evidence to be completely ignored. As mentioned, the proclamation of the resurrection took place very shortly after the events by key church leaders. Paul himself wrote about his own resurrection encounter. The empty tomb is on a solid historical foundation. And only the extreme fringe of biblical scholarship would deny the reality of the disciples' transformation. In short, claiming that the resurrection is a legend is much like attempting to claim that the assassination of Caesar or the majority of the military exploits of Alexander the Great are legendary fabrications.

Another classic explanation was that Jesus recovered from His injuries, and He then walked to the location where His disciples were hiding. Very few today accept this scenario since almost no one ever survived Roman crucifixion. If the commissioned soldiers failed to kill the condemned, they would be executed in the prisoner's place. Even more problematic, if Jesus had stumbled into the presence of the disciples, they would immediately have concluded that He miraculously survived His ordeal, not that He was the risen Savior of the world, with a glorified body. The possibility of His resurrection would never have crossed their minds.

Several other pieces of evidence also make the "swoon theory" completely untenable.[7] The medical reasons are summarized by Dr. Alexander Metherell in an interview conducted by Lee Strobel:

Appealing to history and medicine, to archaeology and even Roman military rules, Metherell had closed every loophole:

Jesus could not have come down from the cross alive. But still, I pushed him further. "Is there any possible way—*any possible way*—that Jesus could have survived this?"

Metherell shook his head and pointed his finger at me for emphasis. "Absolutely not," he said. "Remember that he was already in hypovolemic shock from the massive blood loss even before the crucifixion started. He couldn't possibly have faked his death, because you can't fake the inability to breathe for long. Besides, the spear thrust into his heart would have settled the issue once and for all. And the Romans weren't about to risk their own death by allowing him to walk away alive."[8]

A few other theories are less frequently presented. The oldest is that the disciples stole the body. It originated with the Jewish chief priests immediately after the resurrection (Matthew 28:13). However, virtually no competent scholar has defended it in the past two hundred years since it only explains the empty tomb. One of the more fantastic claims is that Jesus had an unknown identical twin. But even skeptical scholars give this view no credence. The problems of all alternative explanations have been recognized by even some of the most ardent skeptics. For instance, Bart Ehrman comments:

Apologists typically have a field day with such explanations. Anyone who says that the disciples stole the body is attacked for thinking that such moral men who firmly believed what they did could never have done such a thing. Anyone who says that the Romans moved the body is shouted down with claims that they would have produced the body if it had been theirs to produce. Anyone who says that the tomb was empty because the women went to the wrong tomb is maligned for not realizing that it might occur to someone else—for example, an unbeliever—to go to the right tomb and reveal the body. Anyone who claims that Jesus never really died but simply went into a coma and eventually awoke and left the tomb is mocked for thinking that a man who was tortured to within an inch of his life could roll away the stone and appear to his disciples as the Lord of Life, when in fact he would have looked like death warmed over.[9]

HIS RESURRECTION FORETOLD

He then began to teach them that the Son of Man must suffer many things and be rejected by the elders, the chief priests and the teachers of the law, and that he must be killed and after three days rise again.

—Mark 8:31

The resurrection was foretold by the prophets as well as by Jesus Himself. His death was no accident or murder to be solved. In fact, as the Scriptures foretold, He had to suffer and rise again. He spoke of this event in various settings and through many creative and even shocking ways. For instance, He foretold the destruction of the Jewish temple (which happened in AD 70), and then said He would raise it back up in three days, now referring to this body. "Jesus answered them, 'Destroy this temple, and I will raise it again in three days.' [The Jews] replied, 'It has taken forty-six years to build this temple, and you are going to raise it in three days?' But the temple he had spoken of was his body. After he was raised from the dead, his disciples recalled what he had said. Then they believed the Scripture and the words that Jesus had spoken" (John 2:19–22).

Probably one of the most unusual and controversial stories in all of the Bible is the one mentioned in the previous chapter about the prophet Jonah, who was swallowed by a sea creature and then spent three days inside of it. Jesus pointed to this story as a sign of His death and resurrection:

He answered, "A wicked and adulterous generation asks for a sign! But none will be given it except the sign of the prophet Jonah. For as Jonah was three days and three nights in the belly of a huge fish, so the Son of Man will be three days and three nights in the heart of the earth." (Matthew 12:39–40)

The prophets spoke of this resurrection in the Old Testament scriptures, and these prophecies were referenced by the apostles in their preaching:

"But God raised him from the dead, freeing him from the agony of death, because it was impossible for death to keep its hold on him. David said about him:

"'I saw the Lord always before me.
　　Because he is at my right hand,
　　I will not be shaken.
Therefore my heart is glad and my tongue rejoices;
　　my body also will rest in hope,
because you will not abandon me to the realm of the dead,
　　you will not let your holy one see decay.

You have made known to me the paths of life;
you will fill me with joy in your presence.'

"Fellow Israelites, I can tell you confidently that the patriarch
David died and was buried, and his tomb is here to this day.
But he was a prophet and knew that God had promised him
on oath that he would place one of his descendants on his
throne. Seeing what was to come, he spoke of the resurrection
of the Messiah, that he was not abandoned to the realm of the
dead, nor did his body see decay." (Acts 2:24–31)

The resurrection provides the prophetic and historical
foundation for a firm and solid faith. When this is missing, cata-
strophic consequences can result.

THE RESURRECTION IS THE FOUNDATION OF OUR FAITH

Skeptics, such Bart Erhman and Michael Shermer, tell similar
stories of once being fundamentalist Christians who actually
went door-to-door doing personal evangelism. They tell how
their journey to unbelief began when they questioned the absolute inerrancy of Scripture. They were told that this high view of
Scripture was the true foundation of faith. As much as I believe
in the inerrancy and infallibility of Scripture, the ultimate foundation of the faith doesn't rest on that claim. In a conversation
with New Testament scholar Dan Wallace, he concurred that
many times skeptics who were once fundamentalist Christians
merely exchange one form of dogmatism for another.

Jesus' resurrection is the ultimate test for the truth of the Christian faith. The resurrection then supports the Scripture's divine inspiration and reliability, not the other way around. I have seen people thrown into a faith crisis if they discover a difficulty in Scripture that they can't explain. The list of difficulties critics can produce is quite long. While the majority of them can be worked out by patiently and objectively applying the law of noncontradiction or simply the law of common sense, our faith isn't on hold until those kinds of problems are resolved.

Christianity grew because the apostles preached that Christ had been raised from the dead in fulfillment of the Hebrew prophets. His death satisfied the claims of justice for breaking God's law, and His perfect life qualified Jesus to be the Lamb of God, the sacrifice without spot or blemish. The New Testament Gospels and letters of Paul would not be written down for almost two decades, yet the church grew dramatically and quickly in that time. The central core of their message was the reality of the resurrection. While it is a necessary and noble task to defend the authority of Scripture, we must not go beyond what Scripture itself says about the content of the central gospel presentation.

The stories I have heard about how the resurrection saved people's faith from skepticism are many. At nineteen Dr. George Wood was struggling with this very dilemma of wanting to believe that his faith was credible but having difficulty in finding the solid footing he needed. It was when he heard a lecture on the historicity of the resurrection that he found that unshakable foundation. "I now realized that I could trust the words of Jesus because He had been raised from the dead in history."[10] Today he leads the Assemblies of God, a group of some three hundred thousand churches in more than two hundred nations.

HOW THE RESURRECTION AFFECTS OUR UNDERSTANDING OF THE GOSPELS

Historians would never question the reliability of the Gospels if they consistently applied the same standards to them as with other ancient texts. The main reason they deny their reliability is that they reject any claim of the supernatural, particularly Jesus' rising from the dead. Then they must believe that the disciples were so confused about the actual events that delusional fables quickly spread in the early church. However, if Jesus actually rose from the dead, He truly represented God's presence on earth, and the disciples' reports were accurate.

Much follows from this realization. First, Jesus would have anticipated His death and resurrection, so He would have adequately prepared His disciples to accurately pass on His teaching to future generations. In addition, the future authors and collectors of scripture would have been guided by the Holy Spirit to ensure the information was faithfully preserved. One could hardly imagine God passively watching in heaven as Jesus' message was progressively corrupted. Particularly when Jesus Himself promised the apostles that the Holy Spirit would remind them of all He taught, and He would teach them whatever else they needed to understand (John 14:26).

Jesus commissioned His disciples to spread His message to all nations, and He promised He would remain with them until the end (Matthew 28:18–20). Therefore, we can confidently know that they faithfully taught His message and recounted His ministry continuously for decades. They also trained future leaders to pass on that information to the next generation. And those leaders passed the tradition on to the next generation. This process continued well after the Gospels were written and copied throughout the known world. Clement, successor of Peter in Rome, wrote:

> The Apostles received the gospel for us from the Lord Jesus Christ; and Jesus Christ was sent from God. Christ, therefore, is from God, and the Apostles are from Christ. Both of these orderly arrangements, then, are by God's will. Receiving their instructions and being full of confidence on account of the resurrection of our Lord Jesus Christ, and confirmed in faith by the word of God, they went forth in the complete assurance of the Holy Spirit, preaching the good news that the Kingdom of God is coming. Through countryside and city they preached; and they appointed their earliest converts, testing them by the Spirit, to be the bishops and deacons of future believers.[11]

NOT A CIRCULAR ARGUMENT

A common accusation of skeptics is that Christians believe in the resurrection simply because the Bible says it happened. If that claim were true, the logic would then follow like this:

—The Bible is God's Word.
—The Bible says Jesus was raised from the dead.
—Therefore, Jesus was raised from the dead because the Bible says it.

Such an argument would be circular reasoning and logically invalid.

Actually, the argument being made doesn't begin and end with the claim that the Bible is true. It states:

—Jesus was crucified and raised from the dead in history.
—His resurrection validated His identity as the Son of God.
—The New Testament writings are historically reliable and further testify to these facts.
—Therefore, both history and Scripture confirm that Jesus Christ of Nazareth was raised from the dead, three days after His crucifixion.

This is a linear argument, not circular. The beginning premise is that Jesus existed and that His crucifixion by the Roman leader Pontius Pilate is part of the historical record. Therefore, His resurrection is the best explanation of the historical facts that even skeptics recognize as true. The New Testament writings are reliable historical documents and further confirm the crucifixion and the resurrection as real events. They also explain that this supernatural event points to Jesus' identity as the Son of God. The conclusion, therefore, flows from a historical event, not just a random assertion in a religious book, as skeptics like to portray.

Dr. Gary Habermas illustrates the significance of this distinction when giving his talks on the reality of the resurrection. He holds up a Bible and says, "If this Bible is the inerrant, infallible Word of God, Jesus is raised from the dead. If this Bible is not inerrant but still reliable, Jesus is raised from the dead. But what if the Bible is neither reliable nor inerrant? Jesus is still raised from the dead."[12] This is a vital truth to hold on to as you face the skeptical barrage that awaits the believer in Jesus in today's society.

THE SIGNIFICANCE OF THE RESURRECTION

Before we close this important chapter, let's look at an overview of the significance of the resurrection—in other words, what is the impact of this event? History can point to the resurrection as the best explanation of the facts, but it can't tell us fully what they meant. By looking at the Scripture, we gain valuable wisdom into what it really means.

Jesus' Identity Verified

> Paul, a servant of Christ Jesus, called to be an apostle and set apart for the gospel of God—the gospel he promised beforehand through his prophets in the Holy Scriptures regarding his Son, who as to his earthly life was a descendant of David, and who through the Spirit of holiness was appointed the Son of God in power by his resurrection from the dead: Jesus Christ our Lord.
>
> —Romans 1:1–4

The resurrection verified that Jesus indeed was the Son of God. With so many making claims about speaking for God or even being the Messiah, we vitally need our certainty of Christ's identity to be attested to by God.

This fact reminds me of the importance of identity verification. Who we are must be established beyond our own testimony.

We do not show up at the airport and expect to be allowed into a secure area without confirmation of who we are. The resurrection verified who He is. In a world of identity theft and deception, we can have confidence in placing our trust in Jesus Christ. Because Jesus has been raised from the dead, we can trust that His words were true and trustworthy—the very Word of God.

Proof of Life After Death

As I pass through the checkout line at the grocery, I'm amused at the headlines with sensational titles like "New Proof of Life After Death." Near death experiences are a fascinating field of study and have yielded testimony that cannot be dismissed as mere hallucination or a product of an altered mental state. Yet the resurrection of Jesus is unlike any of these claims. After being scourged and tortured, Christ was crucified and buried. After three days, He came back to life as He foretold.

This event gives overwhelming evidence that there is life after death. As Jesus said to His disciples, "I go to prepare a place for you" (John 14:2 NKJV). The fact that heaven exists is based on the testimony of the Son of God. We can have genuine hope and comfort in the fact that our existence does not end with physical death. As the apostle Paul wrote:

When the perishable has been clothed with the imperishable, and the mortal with immortality, then the saying that is written will come true: "Death has been swallowed up in victory."

"Where, O death, is your victory?
Where, O death, is your sting?" (1 Corinthians 15:54–55)

We Are Raised Up Spiritually—Given New Birth

But because of his great love for us, God, who is rich in mercy, made us alive with Christ even when we were dead in transgressions—it is by grace you have been saved. And God raised us up with Christ and seated us with him in the heavenly realms in Christ Jesus.

—Ephesians 2:4–6

Jesus told a religious leader named Nicodemus that he must be born again (John 3:3). Paul promised that if anyone is in Christ, he or she is a new creation (2 Corinthians 5:17). This statement means that we are transformed from within. The resurrection provides the power to raise us up into this new life. We are no longer bound to the dictates of fleshly desires or proclivities. Because the power of the resurrection is available to us, we can live a life that honors and pleases God.

Resurrection Proves the Judgment to Come

Having overlooked the times of ignorance, God is now declaring to men that all people everywhere should repent, because He has fixed a day in which He will judge the world in righteousness . . . having furnished proof to all men by raising Him from the dead.

—Acts 17:30–31 NASB

The resurrection of Jesus is the proof that He is the Son of God and the ultimate Judge, whom we will face at the end of the world. To many, the concept of judgment is too frightening to consider, but ignoring this topic does not dismiss it or make it disappear.

God promised to judge the world through Christ. The fact that there is a day coming when we all will stand before the judgment seat of Christ and give an account of our life bolsters our spiritual immune system to resist evil and choose righteousness.

As we look at the New Testament, this message of the coming judgment was an integral part of the presentation of the early church. While we are called to be merciful and not judgmental of others, we are nevertheless headed for the day of standing before the Lord in eternity. This anticipation should inspire us to give our all to the service of Christ and the work of advancing the gospel.

RESURRECTION WAS THE CENTRAL MESSAGE OF THE EARLY CHURCH

The resurrection was the core of the message that birthed the church in the midst of a hostile culture. There are at least ten significant incidents that incited speeches centering on the resurrection in the book of Acts. These messages were presented in different countries, often to prominent leaders—both religious and secular. Here is an overview:

1. At the Day of Pentecost, Fifty Days After Christ's Crucifixion

"Fellow Israelites, listen to this: Jesus of Nazareth was a man accredited by God to you by miracles, wonders and signs, which God did among you through him, as you yourselves know. This man was handed over to you by God's deliberate plan and foreknowledge; and you, with the help of wicked men, put him to death by nailing him to the cross. But God raised him from the dead, freeing him from the agony of death, because it was impossible for death to keep its hold on him." (Acts 2:22–24)

2. To the Crowds of People Astonished at the Healing of a Lame Man

"The God of Abraham, Isaac and Jacob, the God of our fathers, has glorified his servant Jesus. You handed him over to be killed, and you disowned him before Pilate, though he had decided to let him go. You disowned the Holy and Righteous One and asked that a murderer be released to you. You killed the author of life, but God raised him from the dead. We are witnesses of this." (Acts 3:13–15)

3. When Speaking to the Authorities After the Same Healing

"Then know this, you and all the people of Israel: It is by the name of Jesus Christ of Nazareth, whom you crucified but whom God raised from the dead, that this man stands before you healed." (Acts 4:10)

4. After They Were Threatened by Religious Leaders for Continuing to Speak About Jesus

"The God of our ancestors raised Jesus from the dead—whom you killed by hanging him on a cross. God exalted him to his own right hand as Prince and Savior that he might bring Israel to repentance and forgive their sins. We are witnesses of these things, and so is the Holy Spirit, whom God has given to those who obey him."

When they heard this, they were furious and wanted to put them to death. (Acts 5:30–33)

5. When the Gospel Came to the Gentiles

"God anointed Jesus of Nazareth with the Holy Spirit and power, and . . . he went around doing good and healing all who were under the power of the devil, because God was with him.

"We are witnesses of everything he did in the country of the Jews and in Jerusalem. They killed him by hanging him on a cross, but God raised him from the dead on the third day and caused him to be seen. He was not seen by all the people, but by witnesses whom God had already chosen—by us who ate and drank with him after he rose from the dead. He commanded us to preach to the people and to testify that he is the one whom God appointed as judge of the living and the dead. All the prophets testify about him that everyone who believes in him receives forgiveness of sins through his name." (Acts 10:38–43)

6. In a Jewish Synagogue

"The people of Jerusalem and their rulers did not recognize Jesus, yet in condemning him they fulfilled the words of the prophets that are read every Sabbath. Though they found no proper ground for a death sentence, they asked Pilate to have him executed. When they had carried out all that was written about him, they took him down from the cross and laid him in a tomb. But God raised him from the dead, and for many days he was seen by those who had traveled with him from Galilee to Jerusalem. They are now his witnesses to our people.

"We tell you the good news: What God promised our ancestors he has fulfilled for us, their children, by raising up Jesus. As it is written in the second Psalm:

"'You are my son;
today I have become your Father.'

"God raised him from the dead so that he will never be subject to decay. As God has said,

"'I will give you the holy and sure blessings promised to David.'

"So it is also stated elsewhere:
"'You will not let your holy one see decay.'

"Now when David had served God's purpose in his own generation, he fell asleep; he was buried with his ancestors and his body decayed. But the one whom God raised from the dead did not see decay." (Acts 13:27–37)

7. Introducing the Gospel in the City of Thessalonica

As was his custom, Paul went into the synagogue, and on three Sabbath days he reasoned with them from the Scriptures, explaining and proving that the Messiah had to suffer and rise from the dead. "This Jesus I am proclaiming to you is the Messiah," he said. Some of the Jews were persuaded and joined Paul and Silas, as did a large number of God-fearing Greeks and quite a few prominent women. (Acts 17:2–4)

8. In Athens Among the Intellectual Elite

"In the past God overlooked such ignorance, but now he commands all people everywhere to repent. For he has set a day when he will judge the world with justice by the man he has appointed. He has given proof of this to everyone by raising him from the dead."

When they heard about the resurrection of the dead, some of them sneered, but others said, "We want to hear you again on this subject." (Acts 17:30–32)

9. Before a Governor

"When they came here with me, I did not delay the case, but convened the court the next day and ordered the man to be brought in. When his accusers got up to speak, they did not charge him with any of the crimes I had expected. Instead, they had some points of dispute with him about their own religion and about a dead man named Jesus who Paul claimed was alive." (Acts 25:17–19)

10. Before a King

"But God has helped me to this very day; so I stand here and testify to small and great alike. I am saying nothing beyond what the prophets and Moses said would happen—that the Messiah would suffer and, as the first to rise from the dead, would bring the message of light to his own people and to the Gentiles." (Acts 26:22–23)

As the book of Acts ends, Paul is in Rome, waiting to stand before Caesar. Looking at the clear pattern of what he said to those he spoke to, there is little doubt that he would have told him that Christ had been raised from the dead, making Him the supreme authority in the earth.

In the West, the predominant message is God's grace and love. It was certainly God's love that motivated His sending Jesus to rescue humanity. However, it was His death and resurrection that accomplished this mission. The resurrection, therefore, was the overwhelming theme in the preaching of the apostles, not the love of God. In no way am I trying to marginalize this great love or grace—I'm just trying to show what message caused the church to emerge against all odds in the midst of a hostile Roman empire and a resistant religious system. If we want the results the early church had, we must preach the message they preached.

SUMMARY

This chapter is at the heart of the argument that the Jesus of history is the Christ of faith. Christ's resurrection sets Him apart from all other religious leaders and sets Christianity apart from all other religions. The Scripture offers this as the event that verifies the identity of Jesus and the truth of His words.

Conversely, if one could show that Christ was not raised, then the Christian faith would be proven false.

The best explanation of the facts of Jesus' crucifixion, empty tomb, appearances to His disciples after His death, and the sudden emergence of the Christian faith is that Jesus was raised bodily from the dead. This event was at the core of the message that the early disciples preached and spread to the nations of the world. Its truth and power compelled them out into a hostile Roman empire to declare that Jesus was Lord. It was a message that they would be willing to give their lives for and one that would give life to those who heard and believed.

6

DISPELLING THE MYTHS

The Uniqueness of the Jesus Story

That some modern authors continue to suggest
that the Gospel is based on myth is irresponsible
at best and intentionally deceptive at worst.[1]

—J. ED KOMOSZEWSKI

I'M A LITTLE RELUCTANT TO ADMIT THAT WATCHING late-night comedian Bill Maher is an occasional pastime for me. For one thing, he's my age and reminds me of some of my friends growing up who always had a quick, off-color comment on just about everything. Maher gets paid to say things we would have been thrown out of school for repeating. Times have definitely changed. Another reason for watching is that his show gives a quick glimpse into the objections and conundrums of the skeptical mind.

Unhindered by traditional network censorship (what little is left), he can broadcast his often crude, bombastic ideology while his adoring audience shouts approval. This is very important because in America many decide who's right and who's wrong by who gets the loudest applause. Maher admits that his apparent cleverness is not as off-the-cuff and intuitive as it appears. In one of his books, he acknowledges the incredible team of writers and assistants that help him hone his sharp wit and acerbic speech and fine-tune his attacks against his favorite target: religion.

As smart as his crack team of comedic writers is, they haven't done their homework in terms of biblical history. The main reason is that historical facts can get in the way of a good story, especially when your expressed goal in life is to help end religion.

This is on full display in Maher's 2007 movie *Religulous* (not misspelled), where he showcases his tactic of interviewing religious people, most who certainly don't represent the mainstream of Christian thought. Missing for the most part are academic philosophers and historians. That wouldn't fit his intended narrative that religion is for the unthinking person.

In spite of the incessant, inane anti-God rhetoric, I actually like him. In a strange way his railings against hypocrisy, at times, have bits of truth in them even though most of his rants border on the kind of intolerance of which he accuses religion. One of the central claims of his movie is that the story of Jesus was borrowed from ancient pagan mythology. Maher interviews an assortment of people and asks whether they know a long list of pagan gods and personalities that had stories prior to, as well as similar to, the Jesus story.

Afterward comes a montage of images from various Jesus films. The captions read as follows:

- Written in 1280 BC, the Egyptian book of the dead describes a god, Horus

- Horus is the son of the god Osiris
- Born of a virgin mother
- Was baptized in a river by Anup the Baptizer
- Who was later beheaded
- Like Jesus, Horus was tempted while alone in the desert
- Healed the sick
- Healed the blind
- Cast out demons
- And walked on water
- He raised Asar from the dead
- Asar translates to Lazarus
- Oh yeah, he also had twelve disciples
- Yes, Horus was crucified first
- After three days two women announced
- Horus the savior of humanity had been resurrected

At first glance this list of similarities between Horus, an ancient Egyptian god, and Jesus seems incredible. Maher presents all this information as fact and with the air of how it is common knowledge to all intelligent people. I have been to Egypt and worked with Christian leaders, and their response to such claims has been complete disbelief. "If you made this kind of claim in Egypt, people would think you're crazy," said Egyptian pastor Shaddy Soliman.

First, there is no validity to these claims. None have any real historical basis. They are the academic equivalent to a drive-by shooting—something said to quickly kill someone's faith. I have had conversations on university campuses with students who have bought into this idea that the Jesus story was fabricated or simply plagiarized from other earlier religions. Unfortunately, there is rarely enough time to sit with them and look at the evidence in any objective sense. They assume it must be true because somebody said it was true.

Before we go any further and talk about the roots of this whole notion of the "Jesus myth" and the supposed parallels, let us take a look at Maher's assertions of similarities between Jesus and Horus. Here are a few highlights from some of these preposterous claims.[2]

Description of Horus

First, Horus was a mythical god with the head of a falcon and the body of a man. His mother was Isis and his father Osiris.

The book of the dead

This was a guide to the underworld and a collection of spells to help you after death.

There were many different books of the dead. These so-called parallels were pieced together from a wide range of books. The early Christians would not have had access to any of these writings, so it would have been impossible for them to somehow copy the story or any part of it in the first place.

Born of a virgin

Osiris was killed and dismembered, and his body parts cast into a river. Isis retrieved his genitals and then inseminated herself in order to get pregnant and have the son, Horus.

This was not a virgin birth and does not come close

to matching the biblical account of Jesus' conception in Mary by the power of the Holy Spirit.

Baptized by Anup the Baptizer

This was completely made up by Gerald Massey, an amateur Egyptologist from the nineteenth century. The story was concocted from images of the Pharaohs of Egypt receiving a water cleansing at their coronation. There is no narrative of Horus being baptized.

Healed the sick, healed the blind, cast out demons

Again there were spells in the book of the dead that could supposedly cure people. There is no account of Horus traveling around and personally healing the sick.

Had twelve disciples

This claim also comes from Gerald Massey. It also has no basis in history. Different writings about Horus mention different numbers of people following him, but the number never adds up to twelve. Massey does reference a mural, but the painting does not have Horus as part of it.

Was crucified

Some ancient depictions have Horus with his arms spread apart. But depictions of people with arms spread was not unusual. It certainly does not indicate a Roman crucifixion, particularly since the Egyptians did not use that form of punishment.

Was resurrected

One story does describe Horus dying and then being brought back to life. However, being resuscitated is completely different from the Jewish view of resurrection. In the latter, individuals experience their bodies being completely transformed so they no longer age.

Besides Maher there are other popular websites, movies, and writers that try to pass off this narrative as true. For instance, the movie *Zeitgeist* makes similar accusations that Christianity borrowed from such pagan sources as the ancient worship of the sun, Osiris and Horus, and the Zodiac. These comparisons came from the writings of Dorothy Murdock, who consulted for the script writers. Murdock is a popular writer without any relevant academic training, and her claims have been completely rejected by the scholarly community.

The connections she concocted between Jesus and pagan sources ranged from the very superficial to the completely absurd. For instance, she attempted to relate the number twelve for the number of apostles to the twelve signs of the zodiac. She seemed to have missed the fact that the number of apostles represented the new embodiment of the twelve tribes of Israel. Her other arguments typically stemmed from misreadings of the original source material, use of documents that were written centuries after Jesus lived, or wild speculation.[3]

The problem is that when the average person sees or hears something claiming authoritatively that Christianity "borrowed" from other religions before it, there is very little instruction given to check the credibility of the sources. A quick Google search reveals scores of websites promoting this idea of the Jesus myth.

The problem is that googling something is not the same as researching a topic. The qualified scholars who have thoroughly addressed these claims and found them spurious don't always have their writings located by a search engine.

While the overwhelming number of scholars and academics, whether conservative or liberal, atheist or believer, would accept the historicity of Jesus, there remains a small minority who maintain that Jesus probably didn't exist, and that the Christian story was not original. These kinds of rumors and conspiracy theories are hard to stop once they are articulated and published online and then take on a life of their own. If people have bought into this nonsense, then they respond to anyone trying to convince them that they are mistaken like religious fundamentalists who refuse to listen to anything that challenges their beliefs.

Of all people it is agnostic Bart Erhman who gives the strongest of warnings about this tendency to believe almost anything that someone posts online, "Still, as is clear from the avalanche of sometimes outraged postings on all the relevant Internet sites, there is simply no way to convince conspiracy theorists that the evidence for their position is too thin to be convincing and that the evidence for a traditional view is thoroughly persuasive."[4]

The goal of this chapter, therefore, is to examine the accusation that the Jesus story was borrowed from pagan mythology and show that, in fact, the very opposite is true. If nothing else, you need to know that if anyone borrowed the story, it was the pagan writers who tried to retell their myths to make them sound like the gospel. J. Ed Komoszewski confirms this in *Reinventing Jesus*:

> Only after the rise of Christianity did mystery religions begin
> to look suspiciously like the Christian faith. Once Christianity

became known, many of the mystery cults consciously adopted Christian ideas so that their deities would be perceived to be on a par with Jesus. The shape of the mystery religions prior to the rise of Christianity is vague, ambiguous, and localized. Only by a huge stretch of the imagination, and by playing fast and loose with the historical data, can one see them as having genuine conceptual parallels to the Christian faith of the first century.[5]

That's why we look to dispel the *myth of the myth*. My intent is to bring the light of history to this subject and give you the confidence to help others who are struggling over whether something they heard or read on the Internet about the alleged Jesus myth is actually true. In separating fact from fiction, we can help people find a credible faith in the midst of a sea of confusion and deception.

ROOTS OF THE JESUS MYTH HYPOTHESIS

First, let's look at how this bizarre notion that the early Christians cobbled together the Jesus story from ancient mythology and astrology to construct a new religion. As we learned in chapter 1, doubts about the historical Jesus did not begin to appear until the eighteenth century. Before we go on, we should state the obvious: The fact that Jesus existed was virtually unchallenged for almost seventeen hundred years. As the supernatural aspects of the Gospels began to be reevaluated because of the Enlightenment influences, the only logical alternative to Jesus performing real miracles was that these stories were simply myths or legends. From that position it was easy to then speculate that these so-called miracle stories had been in circulation before the time of Jesus and had merely changed names and clothing to fit the Christian narrative.

Then, in the early nineteenth century, David Strauss, a German theologian, proposed that the miracles of Jesus were merely a mythical expression of the early Christians to try and connect Jesus to the prophecies of the Messiah. Following Strauss, another German, Bruno Bauer, went even further and proposed that the Christian story was similar to ancient stories about the dying and rising gods of the pagan world. "As far back as the 1840s, Bruno Bauer began to publish views that the story of Jesus was rooted in myth. Bauer's greatest influence was on one of his students, Karl Marx, who promoted the view that Jesus never existed. This view eventually became part of communist dogma."[6]

This general belief was fleshed out in more detail in the nineteenth century by authors Kersey Graves and Gerald Massey. Graves argued in his book *The World's Sixteen Crucified Saviors* that numerous stories of crucified savior gods who rose from the dead existed throughout the world. Massey claimed in his book *The Natural Genesis* that the story of the Egyptian god Horus was similar to many details of Jesus in the Gospels. In the twentieth century, very similar claims were propagated by anthropologist Sir James George Frazer in his book *The Golden Bough: A Study in Magic and Religion*. These writings would influence later authors, such as Murdock, to propagate this same line of reasoning. However, the claims of these myth proponents have been thoroughly disproved by leading scholars, particularly the comparisons to the resurrection. Historian Jonathan Smith summarizes:

The category of dying and rising gods, once a major topic of scholarly investigation, must be understood to have been largely a misnomer based on imaginative reconstructions and exceedingly late or highly ambiguous texts. . . . All the deities that have been identified as belonging to the class of dying and rising deities can be subsumed under the two larger classes of disappearing deities or dying deities. In the first case the deities return but have not died; in the second case the gods die but do not return. There is no unambiguous instance in the history of religions of a dying and rising deity.[7]

Despite these refutations, the campaign of misinformation found a following among skeptics willing to accept any explanation for the claims and miracles of Jesus other than the version recorded in the Gospels. Reading these myth proponents reminds one of those who make bold leaps of association that force supposed pieces of a puzzle together that really just don't fit. Using their logic, one could make virtually any claim of association imaginable and be able to "prove" it. Such practices are not real history.

MOTIVES

As we mentioned briefly, part of the motivation for connecting Christianity to pagan myths comes from the denial of the supernatural resulting from the rise of skepticism during the Enlightenment in the eighteenth and nineteenth centuries. Scholars at that time denied the possibility of any supernatural intervention in the world. They also applied evolutionary theory to the study of religion. Specifically, they argued that the understanding of God evolved over time as society developed.[8] As a side note, this process is often the explanation atheists give when they are faced with the evidence of Christianity's positive influence on science and education. Their rebuttal is that though religion "got us started," evolution has taken us beyond our need for any religious or spiritual view of the world. Enlightenment scholars assumed Christianity also evolved from earlier beliefs, so they naturally looked to pagan religions as a source of those developments.

Without attempting to dissect the psychological motivation of those espousing these notions, it is safe to say that their conclusions were not the product of objective historical research. The appearance of these writings in nineteenth-century Germany claiming that the Jesus story was not original should give us pause to consider the motivation of such speculation. The fact that Jesus was Jewish and all the disciples were Jewish produced a desire to change the narrative. The attempts to dismiss the Jewishness of Jesus was clearly a key factor. The fact that Jesus was a first-century Jew is still problematic for the multitudes that harbor bias and anti-Semitic bigotry. "One of the most astonishing features of the quest of the historical Jesus has been the seeming determination of generation after generation of questers to discount or to strip away anything characteristically Jewish from the Jesus tradition. We can explain the underlying logic, even if we can never sympathize with it—the logic of traditional Christian anti-Semitism,"[9] comments James Dunn in *A New Perspective on Jesus*.

However, the primary reason many make such a fantastic claim about Jesus being a mythical being is to dismiss the claims that He makes as Lord of the universe and the ultimate moral authority to whom we are accountable. Think about any sporting match you might attend; at almost every event you find people disdaining the referees. I cannot imagine a more thankless job. Fans on both sides will at some point in the contest hurl insults of the vilest nature at the person in charge of enforcing the rules for daring to penalize their team.

The same can be said of the police. The very sight of a police car can throw you into a panic. Of course, they are a welcome sight when you need them, but they represent the reality of the law of the land. People don't mind acknowledging the Creator, just as long as God keeps His distance from us, until we really need Him. The thought of a personal God who knows our thoughts and actions and will call us to account is unnerving. Even though Jesus came and sacrificed His life on our behalf to demonstrate His love, the fact that there is a judgment to come is not a pleasant thought. Denying these realities might prove comforting to skeptics. But as Richard Dawkins likes to say, "Just because a thought is unpleasant doesn't mean it isn't true."

CHRISTIANITY ROOTED IN JUDAISM

If there's anything in this book that should be crystal clear to you, it's that Jesus was Jewish. Before we look at the various pagan deities that have been proposed as alleged forerunners to Jesus, it is necessary to understand that in Israel, Christianity rose out of the very soil of Judaism, not because of pagan mythology. James Dunn concurs with this thought:

Nevertheless, looking at Jesus within the context of the Judaism of his time remains a more plausible line of search than starting with the intent of wrenching him out from that context. By noting what the characteristics are of Jewish practice and belief, we can infer, unless we have indications to the contrary, that Jesus shared these characteristics. A basic list would include the fact that he was circumcised, that he was brought up to say the Shema, to respect the Torah, to attend the synagogue, to observe the Sabbath. In addition, Sanders has offered a list of what he describes as "almost indisputable facts" about Jesus: that his mission mainly operated round the towns and villages of Galilee.[10]

William Lane Craig affirms the same in *Reasonable Faith*, as we see in the following statement:

Here we see one of the major shifts in New Testament studies over the last century, what I earlier flagged as the Jewish reclamation of Jesus. Scholars came to realize that pagan mythology is simply the wrong interpretive context for understanding Jesus of Nazareth. Evans has called this shift the "Eclipse of Mythology" in Life of Jesus research. Jesus and his disciples were first-century Palestinian Jews, and it is against that background that they must be understood. The spuriousness of the alleged parallels is just one indication that pagan mythology is the wrong interpretive context for understanding the disciples' belief in Jesus' resurrection.[11]

If history means anything, it is clear that it was not the Christians stealing the pagans' stories but the other way around. As Dr. Craig Keener states:

Even apart from this observation, bodily resurrection was a Palestinian Jewish idea. It is difficult to conceive of a rapidly hellenizing Gentile church preaching a dying-and-rising mystery deity triggering Palestinian Jewish Jesus people to adopt a pagan idea and then modify it in a Palestinian Jewish direction (including the specifically Jewish language of "resurrection"). It is far more likely that later Gentiles attracted to a growing Jewish cult would have adopted and transformed a Palestinian Jewish understanding of the resurrection.[12]

SOURCES, SCHOLARS, AND SUBSTANCE

In a political season many candidates throw their hats into the ring, so to speak, and run for office. As time goes on, the field begins to narrow, and you find a few emerge as the real contenders to be elected. Similarly, skeptics often attempt to quickly present a long list of so-called Jesus parallels, but a few are commonly cited as leading contenders. The following section describes some of the most popularly cited myth sources and shows the flimsiness of the supporting arguments. There are three key principles to keep in mind as these parallels are examined: sources, scholars, and substance.

Sources

What is glaringly missing time and time again are any original sources for these imaginative claims. Skeptics typically make assertions out of thin air, or they quote earlier writers who made the same claim but also failed to cite any original sources. Bart Ehrman agrees:

The authors provide no evidence for their claims concerning the standard mythology of the godmen. They cite no sources from the ancient world that can be checked. It is not that they have provided an alternative interpretation of the available evidence. They have not even cited the available evidence. And for good reason. No such evidence exists.[13]

It is incredible that virtually none of the scrutiny and verification is applied to the myth theories by the skeptics that they demand the Gospels be subjected to. The result is a massive distinction between the material that is genuine and the other material that is clearly fiction.

Scholars

Second, arguments come from popular writers without any relevant academic credentials. Or they represent opinions that have been rejected by virtually all respected scholars. In particular, myth proponents often argue that virtually all of the New Testament writings are completely unhistorical. They believe they were fabricated to serve the agendas of the later writers. For instance, Richard Carrier, one of the few myth proponents with relevant credentials, stated, "The authors of the Gospels clearly had no interest in any actual historical data."[14]

This is a scandalous statement in light of history. No competent historian believes, as detailed in chapter 2, that the New Testament is completely devoid of any historical content. In contrast, the writings (as described in chapter 3) are some of the best from that era, supported by historical and archaeological evidence. In addition, many New Testament details originally believed by skeptics to be unhistorical were eventually proven to be accurate, such as the existence of the city of Nazareth and the Pool of Siloam. In order for myth proponents to argue their views, they have to ignore the most recent archaeological discoveries and reject virtually all standards of sound historical study.

Substance

Finally, the myth proponents suffer from what Dan Wallace described as "parallelomania." Namely, they tend to argue that certain similarities between pagan sources and Christianity prove that Christians copied the pagan stories. However, the parallels invariably lack any real substance. They are either too superficial, or they come from documents that postdate Christianity by centuries.

Even if the parallels were earlier and far more similar, they still would not prove copying. Many remarkable coincidental similarities exist between different religions and between different historical events. One of the most striking examples is the similarity between the assassination of Abraham Lincoln and that of John F. Kennedy. Numerous details perfectly coincide:

- Abraham Lincoln was elected to Congress in 1846. John F. Kennedy was elected to Congress in 1946.
- Abraham Lincoln was elected president in 1860. John F. Kennedy was elected president in 1960.
- *Lincoln* and *Kennedy* each have seven letters.
- Lincoln had a secretary name Kennedy; Kennedy had a secretary named Lincoln.
- Both were married in their thirties to twenty-four-year-old, socially prominent girls who could speak fluent French.

- Both presidents dealt with civil rights movements for African Americans.
- Both presidents were assassinated in the back of the head, while sitting next to their wives, on a Friday before a major holiday.
- Both their assassins were known by three names consisting of fifteen letters (John Wilkes Booth, Lee Harvey Oswald).
- Oswald shot Kennedy from a warehouse and was captured in a theater; Booth shot Lincoln in a theater and was captured in a warehouse.
- Both assassins were shot and killed with a Colt revolver days after they assassinated the president, before they could be brought to trial.
- Both presidents were succeeded by vice presidents named Johnson; both Johnsons were from the South, born in 1808 and 1908 respectively.[15]

Despite this remarkable list, no one believes that one assassination was a mythical retelling of the other. For no evidence exists that copying took place, and the accounts of both assassinations rest on solid historical foundations. Similarly, not a shred of evidence exists that the early Christians were influenced by any of the stories about pagan mythical or historical figures. And the time frame between the events and the writing of the Gospels and letters was far too short for myths to have developed since eyewitnesses were still alive. "There was not enough time for legends to accrue significantly. Ever since D. F. Strauss broached his theory that the Gospels' accounts of Jesus' life and resurrection are the products of legendary and mythical development, the unanswered difficulty for this viewpoint has been that the temporal and geographical distance between the events and the accounts is insufficient to allow for such extensive development."[16]

Finally, the core Jesus story and even many minor details are supported by the strongest historical evidence. Therefore, no justification exists for skeptics to continue to present the myth argument, except to justify their own desire to discredit Christianity.

OTHER PARALLELS TO CHRIST?

These described problems can be clearly seen by examining the claims related to the most popular Jesus-parallel candidates.

Krishna

One of the first candidates mentioned by Bill Maher in his documentary was the deity Krishna, who is one of the most popular Hindu gods. In Hinduism, Krisha is believed to be the incarnation of the god Vishnu. He is commonly depicted in Eastern art as a blue child. As mentioned, Maher listed several specific parallels between Krisha's story and Jesus, including the virgin birth, working as a carpenter (the actual claim is that Krishna's father worked as a carpenter), and being baptized in a river.

These same assertions have been made by the usual suspects of myth proponents. They also claim that Krishna was crucified, rose from the dead, and shared with Jesus numerous other commonalities. This small circle of writers and fringe scholars promote books without references to any primary sources, which is understandable since none of their claims have any basis in reality. For instance, the birth narrative in the Hindu text states that Krishna's mother already had seven children before delivering him, so she certainly was not a virgin. The birth stories also do not explicitly mention that the mother was divinely impregnated.[17] Likewise, the claim about Krishna's being born of a carpenter was simply made up. His father was a nobleman.[18] Nor do any records exist of his being baptized in a river. Likewise, no texts claim that Krishna was crucified or resurrected. He was, instead, killed mistakenly by a hunter named Jara, and then his soul left his body.[19] The only identified parallels of any substance come from texts that were written hundreds of years after the Gospels, when Hindus began copying Christianity.[20]

To summarize, the claims about the parallels between Jesus and Krishna match those with Horus, in that they fall into the categories mentioned previously:

- Similarities so superficial that they represent characteristics common to many religions, such as the presence of miracles. Therefore, they provide no evidence of copying.
- Parallels that are more substantial are based on gross misrepresentations of the original texts or simply made up.
- Parallels that are substantial and based on legitimate historical sources were written long after the first century. The only copying would have been pagans borrowing from the Christians.

Mithras

The second common copycat candidate is Mithras, who was worshiped in the Roman Empire by the followers of the mystery religion known as Mithraism. Little is known about this religion since no major writings have survived. Most of our knowledge comes from shrines.[21] What has been suggested is that Mithras was seen as the god of light, who offered salvation to his followers. One of his most memorable acts was slaying a bull, which was the source of the religion's ritual of pouring the blood of a bull over worshipers. Skeptics often connect this rite to the Christian belief in the blood of Jesus cleansing Christians of their sins. Myth proponents, such as Maher, have also argued that several other details about Jesus were copied from Mithras, including being born on December 25, performing miracles, resurrecting on the third day, and being known by several of the same titles of Jesus, such as the way, the truth, and the life.

As with Horus and Krishna, the truly striking similarities between Jesus and Mithras, such as the resurrection, were simply made up.[22] And the actual similarities are superficial at best. For instance, the use of blood in worship is a feature of many religions in the ancient world. Even more problematic is the issue of dates. Mithraism did not take root in the Roman Empire until the late first century. And the earliest documents describing it were written more than a century after the completion of the Christian gospels. Therefore, any borrowing of ideas at that time would have been the followers of Mithras copying from the Christians. However, respected scholars of Mithras do not believe either religion influenced the other. "After almost 100 years of unremitting labor, the conclusion appears inescapable that neither Mithraism nor Christianity proved to be an obvious and direct influence upon the other in the development and demise or survival of either religion. Their beliefs and practices are well accounted for by their most obvious origins and there is no need to explain one in terms of the other."[23]

Osiris

Osiris was said to preside over the soul in judgment. Osiris is also the husband of Isis, one of the most popular Egyptian deities. Skeptics often argue the Osiris myth is one of the main sources behind the Christian belief in the resurrection. They also attempt to connect Osiris's and Jesus' roles in judgment of the dead. Some argue Osiris was the source of several other significant details claimed about Jesus, such as His baptism, being born on December 25, His title of "Good Shepherd," His instituting a eucharist-like sacred meal, and His death atoning for sin. However, these assertions have been rejected by all respected Osiris authorities. New Testament scholar J. Ed Komoszewski summarizes:

> According to the most common version of the myth, Osiris was murdered by his brother who then sank the coffin containing Osiris's body into the Nile river. Isis discovered the body and returned it to Egypt. But her brother-in-law once again gained access to the body, this time dismembering it into fourteen pieces which he scattered widely. Following a long search, Isis recovered each part of the body . . . Sometimes those telling the story are satisfied to say that Osiris came back to life, even though such language claims far more than the myth allows. Some writers go even further and refer to the alleged "resurrection" of Osiris.[24]

Clearly, the alleged similarities between Jesus and Osiris presented by myth proponents are extreme exaggerations or complete figments of their imaginations. The resurrection of Jesus has little in common with Osiris's reassembly by Isis. And as scholar Ronald Nash comments, "The fate of Osiris's coffin in the Nile is as relevant to baptism as the sinking of Atlantis.[25]

Even skeptics such as Bart Ehrman have felt compelled to challenge such irresponsible assertions. For instance, he critiques authors Timothy Freke and Peter Gandy, who repeated many of these claims in their books.

What, for example, is the proof that Osiris was born on December 25 before three shepherds? Or that he was crucified? And that his death brought atonement for sin? Or that he returned to life on earth by being raised from the dead? In fact, no ancient source says any such thing about Osiris (or about the other gods). But Freke and Gandy claim that this is common knowledge. And they "prove" it by quoting other writers from the nineteenth and twentieth centuries who said so. But these writers too do not cite any historical evidence. This is all based on assertion, believed by Freke and Gandy simply because they read it somewhere. This is not serious historical scholarship.[26]

Dishonorable Mention

Several other examples are cited less frequently as sources for Christian copying. One person of interest is Apollonius, who, unlike our previous examples, was a real historical figure. He was a Greek philosopher from the town of Tyana in the Roman province of Cappadocia. He lived around the time of Jesus, and he is claimed to have taught disciples, performed miracles, and appeared to witnesses after his death. These parallels are truly striking. However, they come from a biography written by a philosopher named Philostratus in the third century. So ample time was provided between his death and the writing of the biography for legendary accounts to have developed. In addition, by that time the Christian church had become well established throughout the Roman Empire, so Philostratus likely copied from the Gospels.

Another source occasionally cited is the god Dionysius. He is claimed to be born of a virgin on December 25,[27] changed water into wine, have a triumphant entry riding upon a donkey, have followers worship him by eating bread and drinking wine, be crucified, and rise from the dead. As with the other candidates, these purported similarities are distortions of the original texts or simply made up. For instance, he was the god of wine, but no record exists of wine being used in worship that even remotely resembles the Christian story.[28] Again, the parallels are primarily projections of the minds of those who have already denied Jesus with their hearts.

Summary

The story of the life, death, and resurrection of Jesus was not borrowed from pagan mythology. The very fact that something this absurd has to be addressed demonstrates how shallow the discussion has become in terms of the real facts surrounding the gospel and the implications for every person on the planet.

The roots of Christianity are in the Jewish faith. Jesus was Jewish and came in fulfillment of the Hebrew prophets who spoke about the Messiah. His miracles were not magic tricks or written in mythological language, but pointed people to the redemptive purposes of God and their opportunity to be a part.

Ironically, the copying was not early Christians borrowing from ancient Egyptian, Greek, or Persian stories, but the other way around. The enormous success and growth of early Christianity provoked proponents of mystery religions to retell their story with Christian imagery and themes.

7

JESUS THE MESSIAH

Son of Man, Son of God

There is no other interpretation that fits the facts
of history and the message of Scripture—Jesus
Christ of Nazareth is the promised Messiah.[1]
—DR. STEPHEN C. MEYER

THE HUMANIST MANIFESTO WAS FIRST WRITTEN IN 1933 and laid out a secular vision of how we could end racism, poverty, and war, and bring lasting peace and prosperity to the world. It referred to humanism as a "new religion" that would produce a deity-less religious movement. The Humanist Manifesto II, written in 1973, was an emancipation proclamation against God—more specifically, freedom from the belief that God would be the source of salvation for humanity. It states, "No Deity will save us, we must save ourselves." The assertion that we can be our own salvation is a belief—a faith system. The sad reality is that there is no real evidence that we can trust ourselves to accomplish such an elusive and formidable task. Humanity can bring dramatic solutions to many of life's problems. We can fight cancer, heart disease, hunger, and pollution. We can turn around failing companies, rebuild ruined cities, and restore hope to regions devastated by natural disasters. But can we change the deepest problems in the human soul?

When it comes to our moral behavior, it seems we have conceded that the battle against our genetics is futile. If our sexual impulses and desires should be accepted and not resisted or repressed, then why not legitimize every other instinct and proclivity? As atheist Richard Dawkins said, "We are simply a product of our DNA and we dance to its music."[2] In fact, skeptics such as Sam Harris go as far as to say that there is no such thing as free will and that our actions are determined.[3] If that's the case, then we are in deeper trouble than we've ever imagined.

In the nineteenth century many had a sense of hope that society would naturally evolve into a better and better state through science, education, and reason alone. Leading thinkers had taken the theory of evolution and turned it into an all-encompassing worldview, which they attempted to use as a road map for not only the improvement of humans physically, but mentally and morally as well. During the infamous Scopes "Monkey Trial," more than ninety years ago in Dayton County, Tennessee, the *New York Times* printed an editorial stating that evolution, devoid of any influence from a creator, offered the only hope of progress for the human soul. "If man has evolved, it is inconceivable that the process should stop and leave him in his present imperfect state. Specific creation has no such promise for man."[4]

The greatest need for change is in the human soul. Yet where will this change come from? The concept of survival of the fittest means that nature selects the characteristics that help individuals survive and reproduce. From that perspective, where do character traits such as unselfish love and self-sacrifice come from? The reality is that apart from the Holy Spirit's work in us, we are simply at the mercy of our genes, our fleshly proclivities, and societal pressures. Such a belief naturally leads to an existential despair, which was expressed by biblical writers who doubted the human condition could ever improve. "I have seen all the things that are done under the sun; all of them are meaningless, a chasing after the wind. What is crooked cannot be straightened" (Ecclesiastes 1:14–15).

The real story of humanity is that, left to ourselves, we have proven to not be too good at the salvation business. For many technological breakthroughs, the same technology designed for good can become an instrument for evil. The twentieth century witnessed some of the greatest atrocities conducted by would-be saviors who openly rejected the God of the Bible. Countless millions were slaughtered under such anti-Christian regimes as those led by Stalin, Mao, Pol Pot, Hitler (a neopagan), and Idi Amin. As mentioned, the root problem is ultimately spiritual, and it resides deep within the human spirit.

In spite of the pretenses of science or the political process as being the source of our hope, we are in desperate need of God's help and intervention. The message of Scripture is in essence a revelation of the path that takes us from darkness to light and from despair to hope. Just as there are physical laws that explain how the universe works, there are spiritual laws that help us understand the inner world and how it works. Sigmund Freud tried to explain the science behind human thought and emotion, but he failed to do so for one simple reason. He never acknowledged that the soul had a Creator, so he attempted to explain how we are subconsciously driven to act, not how we should choose to act.

God revealed throughout Scripture how we were meant to live, much as the manufacturer of a car provides an instruction manual that explains how to properly operate and maintain the vehicle. When those laws are violated or ignored, there are consequences. In particular, we cease to behave for the maximum good of ourselves and others. The quandary is that humans have a driving tendency to act in ways that completely defy the way we were intended to live.

THE MESSAGE IS CLEAR: WE NEED A SAVIOR

Because we so desperately need a Savior, we can be so easily taken in by those who promise to fix our problems, heal our wounds, and bring lasting peace in our world. We fall for almost anything that promises us relief from our pain.

The idea that we need salvation started in the beginning of human history. From the time evil asserted its influence, the cry for help rose from the depths of our souls. The very first humans chose to disobey the very simple law that God had given them, so they immediately suffered the pain of the consequent separation that sin brings. Why did God give them the chance to fail? That is the essence of being human—having a real choice to do good or evil.

From that early time the planet has reeled from the self-inflicted wounds of a people making wrong choices. However, at key moments in history, when all seemed lost, God provided a way of escape for those who trusted in Him. The story of Noah building an ark for the salvation of his family; the Lord instructing Moses to put the blood of a lamb over the doorposts of the Israelites' dwellings so that the angel of death would *pass over*, sparing their lives; and the miraculous passage through the Red Sea by the freed Hebrew slaves all tell the story of God's deliverance from evil and oppression. Repeatedly the great King David would praise God for His salvation from his enemies and the many escapes from death he was given.

I love you, LORD, my strength.

The LORD is my rock, my fortress and my deliverer;
    my God is my rock, in whom I take refuge,
    my shield and the horn of my salvation, my stronghold.

I called to the LORD, who is worthy of praise,
    and I have been saved from my enemies. (Psalm 18:1–3)

God not only created the universe, but He is involved in the affairs of humanity. Though there is pain and suffering, deliverance is available. The ultimate manifestation of this salvation would be the appearance of the embodiment of that salvation in human form.

THE MESSIAH

"The Messiah" in Hebrew is *Ha Mashiach*. The same word in Greek is *Christ*, or "Anointed One." It symbolized the anointed priest that had been set apart for God's purposes. In the Old Testament, the Messiah was an anointed leader who would be a descendant of King David who would deliver the Jewish people from their enemies.

The Hebrews expected a human leader who would deliver them from their human oppressors and usher in the kingdom of God on earth politically. They had little idea that the Messiah would be the incarnate presence of God on earth, and they especially did not expect Him to be executed by the very enemies they believed He would vanquish. However, Jesus came to deliver us from our real enemies, the spiritual forces that have kept the human race in bondage. External liberty is worthless without inner freedom.

Jesus would announce this goal as His mission in His inaugural message. After He was baptized in the Jordan River, He returned to Nazareth, where He had been brought up, entered the synagogue, and read from the prophet Isaiah. Here is the account of this incident:

> He went to Nazareth, where he had been brought up, and on the Sabbath day he went into the synagogue, as was his custom. He stood up to read, and the scroll of the prophet Isaiah was handed to him. Unrolling it, he found the place where it is written:
>
> "The Spirit of the Lord is on me,
>> because he has anointed me
>> to proclaim good news to the poor.
> He has sent me to proclaim freedom for the prisoners
>> and recovery of sight for the blind,
> to set the oppressed free,
>> to proclaim the year of the Lord's favor."

Then he rolled up the scroll, gave it back to the attendant and sat down. The eyes of everyone in the synagogue were fastened on him. He began by saying to them, "Today this scripture is fulfilled in your hearing." (Luke 4:16–21)

After reading this prophetic, Messianic passage, He uttered the startling statement that He was fulfilling that Scripture "today." This graphically demonstrates that Jesus not only saw Himself as the fulfillment of the prophets' words but that His mission would be to preach the gospel, heal the sick, and set the spiritually oppressed free. In fact, He embarked immediately to cast out demons and to perform healings and other miracles.

It is this same ministry that He is carrying out today in our generation through His followers. The message that Jesus is the Christ (Messiah) does not advance through violence or force. In fact, those who have forced others into some kind of contrived obedience were condemned by Jesus and called out as false prophets. Instead, the message of Christ goes forth in love and power. This gospel, or good news, is so powerful that it caused the world to be turned upside down two thousand years ago—it can do the same today.

PREPARING THE WAY

The appearance of the Messiah would be unquestionably the most significant moment in human history, so much so that a prophet was sent ahead of time to prepare the people for what was to come. He was called John the Baptist, and historians acknowledge he not only existed, but he preached and ministered in the desert regions of Israel. All four gospels speak of John in this role of preparing the way for the Messiah. John's ministry was foretold by the Hebrew prophets. Malachi prophesied almost four hundred years earlier:

"See, I will send you the prophet Elijah to you before that great and dreadful day of the LORD comes. He will turn the hearts of the parents to their children, and the hearts of the children to their parents; or else I will come and strike the land with total destruction." (Malachi 4:5–6)

This scripture is not speaking of reincarnation, but rather God would send someone with the same kind of anointing and message as Elijah. The prophet Isaiah would speak of John as well, around six hundred years before he appeared:

A voice of one calling:
"In the wilderness prepare
   the way for the LORD;
make straight in the desert
   a highway for our God.
Every valley shall be raised up,
   every mountain and hill made low;
the rough ground shall become level,
   the rugged places a plain." (Isaiah 40:3–4)

John's ministry prepared the hearts and minds of people by calling them to repentance and turning them from their wickedness. When the angel Gabriel told John's parents about his coming birth and future ministry, he said,

> "He will bring back many of the people of Israel to the Lord their God. And he will go on before the Lord, in the spirit and power of Elijah, to turn the hearts of the parents to their children and the disobedient to the wisdom of the righteous—to make ready a people prepared for the Lord." (Luke 1:16–17)

This proclamation points to the exceptional nature of his calling. He wasn't the forerunner for an earthly king or leader but for the Lord Himself. As he was preaching, he was asked if he was the Messiah. He denied it and then declared that the Messiah would come after him:

> Now this was John's testimony when the Jewish leaders in Jerusalem sent priests and Levites to ask him who he was. He did not fail to confess, but confessed freely, "I am not the Messiah."
>
> "I baptize with water," John replied, "but among you stands one you do not know. He is the one who comes after me, the straps of whose sandals I am not worthy to untie."
>
> This all happened at Bethany on the other side of the Jordan, where John was baptizing.
>
> The next day John saw Jesus coming toward him and said, "Look, the Lamb of God, who takes away the sin of the world!" (John 1:19–20, 26–29)

The critical point to grasp is that recognizing the Messiah requires the right spiritual condition as much as acknowledging the facts surrounding His identity. Just because you know Jesus is the Christ doesn't mean you believe in Him to the point of submitting your life and destiny to His leadership and authority. John called people to humble themselves and recognize their need for a Savior. Then, and only then, would they stop trusting in themselves and their idols and remedies of the age and look to God's promise of deliverance on His terms, not their own.

WHAT DID JESUS SAY ABOUT HIMSELF?

The woman said, "I know that Messiah" (called Christ) "is coming. When he comes, he will explain everything to us." Then Jesus declared, "I, the one speaking to you—I am he."

—John 4:25–26

Jesus at times was evasive about His identity as the Messiah since the Jewish people had misconceptions about His role. At other times He was very straightforward about who He was. The account of Jesus and a woman from Samaria gives us a remarkable exchange where His identity was openly revealed. Of all people to confide in, you would probably not guess it would be a woman who had been married five times and was currently living with someone out of wedlock. Yet Jesus spoke directly to her about Him being the Messiah.

As we mentioned earlier, He asked His disciples, "Who do you say that I am?" The apostle Peter spoke out, "You are the Christ, the son of the living God." Jesus answered him not with a correction or rebuke for such a blasphemous set of statements but called him "blessed" for understanding His role. That same blessing comes to us when we grasp this seminal truth about Jesus. Jesus' identity as Messiah was also recognized by the apostle Paul. Craig Keener commented, "Paul, our earliest extant NT writer, sometimes uses 'Christ' virtually as Jesus' surname; the idea of Jesus as 'Messiah' must certainly predate Paul. Paul's language may suggest that the entire Judean Jesus movement that he knew considered Jesus as 'Christ.'"[5]

It is impossible to read the Gospels or Paul and come away with the impression that Jesus of Nazareth thought of Himself as a mere man. Jesus said much about Himself that would have been outlandish if He were just a man.

"I am the light of the world."
—John 8:12

"Heaven and earth will pass away, but my words will never pass away."
—Mark 13:31

"For where two or three are gathered together in My name, I am there in the midst of them."
—Matthew 18:20 NKJV

The prophets who spoke for God prefaced their statements with the phrase, "Thus says the Lord." But when Jesus spoke, He didn't say, "Thus says the Lord," but instead He made comments such as "Truly I say to you." He spoke in such terms because the Lord was speaking.

JESUS DEMONSTRATED HE IS THE MESSIAH

The miracles He performed and the extraordinary signs and wonders pointed to His identity as the Christ. In all of human history there has been no one who has come close to the unbelievable works of Jesus. The only ancient accounts that are vaguely similar were written about figures who had been dead for centuries, so they were only legends. Feeding thousands of people from a few loaves and fish, walking on water, and raising the dead were works beyond human imagination. In fact, one of His most incredible signs was quieting the storm on the Sea of Galilee. This act of calming the seas harked back to God's authority over the waters in Genesis.

Skeptics who don't accept the possibility of supernatural phenomena try to eliminate the miracles of Jesus and focus on His ethics and teaching. But the following He gathered didn't result from a teaching seminar on the Galilean hillside but from the news of His mighty works. It was His miracles that drew the concern of the religious establishment because they pointed to His being the Messiah.

When He did teach, He taught with authority. A prime example was when He not only taught the law of Moses but upgraded it in terms of raising the standard of what it meant:

> "You have heard that it was said to the people long ago, 'You shall not murder, and anyone who murders will be subject to judgment.' But I tell you that anyone who is angry with a brother or sister will be subject to judgment. Again, anyone who says to a brother or sister, 'Raca,' is answerable to the

court. And anyone who says, 'You fool!' will be in danger of the fire of hell." (Matthew 5:21–22)

Dr. William Lane Craig agreed that this demonstrated Jesus' unique sense of His divine authority. "But it's not just that Jesus placed His personal authority on par with that of the divine law. More than that, He adjusted the law on His own authority."[6]

Another example of this authority is His forgiving of sins. To tell people that their sins were forgiven was to act directly as God alone should act. One of my favorite stories in Scripture is recorded in the gospel of Mark. A group of men were trying to transport their paralyzed friend into a crowded house where Jesus was teaching in hopes of his being healed. When they could not enter the front door, they climbed up on the roof, tore a hole through, and then lowered their friend down in front of Jesus. I start smiling when I think of everyone staring at the ceiling as this stretcher was lowered into the room.

> A few days later, when Jesus again entered Capernaum, the people heard that he had come home. They gathered in such large numbers that there was no room left, not even outside the door, and he preached the word to them. Some men came, bringing to him a paralyzed man, carried by four of them. Since they could not get him to Jesus because of the crowd, they made an opening in the roof above Jesus by digging through it and then lowered the mat the man was lying on. When Jesus saw their faith, he said to the paralyzed man, "Son, your sins are forgiven."
>
> Now some teachers of the law were sitting there, thinking

to themselves, "Why does this fellow talk like that? He's blaspheming! Who can forgive sins but God alone?"

Immediately Jesus knew in his spirit that this was what they were thinking in their hearts, and he said to them, "Why are you thinking these things? Which is easier: to say to the paralyzed man, 'Your sins are forgiven,' or to say, 'Get up, take your mat and walk'? But I want you to know that the Son of Man has authority on earth to forgive sins." So he said to the man, "I tell you, get up, take your mat and go home." He got up, took his mat and walked out in full view of them all. This amazed everyone and they praised God, saying, "We have never seen anything like this!" (Mark 2:1–12)

The fact that He directly forgave people's sins demonstrated that He believed He had the authority to do so. No prophet before Him had ever dared to directly tell people their sins were forgiven. Even Moses would pray and ask God to forgive the people, but it was God alone who granted the forgiveness.

PROPHECIES OF A MESSIAH

"All the prophets testify about him that everyone who believes
in him receives forgiveness of sins through his name."

—Acts 10:43

Jesus' advent was the fulfillment of prophecies that God had spoken through the prophets for centuries. "God gave a great number of prophecies about the Messiah for at least two reasons. First, it would make identifying the Messiah obvious. And second, it would make an imposter's task impossible."[7] There are many prophecies that find their fulfillment in Christ. Here we highlight a few.[8] If these seven were the only ones, they would be enough:

1. *The Suffering Servant*

The most graphic and compelling prophecy about the Messiah that points to Jesus of Nazareth is found in the book of Isaiah chapter 53. This passage is referenced several times in the New Testament. It is mentioned not only in the Gospels, when speaking of Christ and His ministry, but also in the book of Acts, when the Ethiopian official questioned Phillip about its meaning (Acts 8:32–33). The passage was decisive in the Ethiopian's journey to faith in Christ as it has been for millions since:

> Surely he took up our pain
> > and bore our suffering,
> yet we considered him punished by God,
> > stricken by him, and afflicted.
> But he was pierced for our transgressions,
> > he was crushed for our iniquities;
> the punishment that brought us peace was on him,
> > and by his wounds we are healed.
> We all, like sheep, have gone astray,
> > each of us has turned to our own way;
> and the LORD has laid on him
> > the iniquity of us all.
>
> He was oppressed and afflicted,
> > yet he did not open his mouth;

he was led like a lamb to the slaughter,
> and as a sheep before its shearers is silent,
> so he did not open his mouth.
By oppression and judgment he was taken away.
> Yet who of his generation protested?
For he was cut off from the land of the living;
> for the transgression of my people he was punished.
He was assigned a grave with the wicked,
> and with the rich in his death,
though he had done no violence,
> nor was any deceit in his mouth.

Yet it was the LORD's will to crush him and cause him to suffer,
> and though the LORD makes his life an offering for sin,
he will see his offspring and prolong his days,
> and the will of the LORD will prosper in his hand.
After he has suffered,
> he will see the light of life and be satisfied;
by his knowledge my righteous servant will justify many,
> and he will bear their iniquities. (Isaiah 53:4–11)

This is one of the most important passages in all of Scripture because of its stunning prophetic picture of the work of Christ. It is filled with references that point to Christ as the Messiah. Space doesn't permit a full exposition of this passage of Scripture, written almost six hundred years before Christ, but a careful reading gives numerous comparisons to the life and death of Jesus. Most important are the verses that state He was "pierced for our transgressions" and "crushed for our iniquities" and that He was "cut off from the land of the living; for the transgression of my people." These statements allude to Jesus being crucified for our sins. Other references are made to Jesus being put to death alongside wicked men but being buried in the tomb of a wealthy man, Joseph of Arimathea.

Even before Jesus came, many rabbis recognized this passage pointed to the promised Messiah. Up unto this day, Isaiah 53 has proven decisive in many Jewish people's embracing Jesus as the Messiah. However, after Jesus came some Jewish commentators rejected it as referring to the Messiah but, instead, claimed it referred solely to the nation of Israel. Their arguments, however, rest on a faulty understanding of the passage's context and interpretation. The most accurate reading clearly points to a future Messiah who precisely matches Jesus' life, death, and resurrection.[9]

2. Messiah's Birthplace

Jesus' birth in Bethlehem is widely accepted yet not without skeptical challenge. It is not difficult to understand why. The fact that the place of His birth would be foretold adds to the credibility of His true identity as the Messiah. Jesus didn't just appear on the scene, making bold statements about Himself. The details of His life were described in advance. God is concerned with not only the big events but also the details.

> "But you, Bethlehem Ephrathah,
>> though you are small among the clans of Judah,
> out of you will come for me
>> one who will be ruler over Israel,
> whose origins are from of old,
>> from ancient times." (Micah 5:2)

This prophecy is very specific about the "ruler" that would come forth from "ancient times" and the place of His birth. King David—in the promised lineage of the Messiah—was also from this very city. The name *Bethlehem* means "house of bread." Out of the house of bread would come the Bread of Life.

3. The One They Pierced

Zechariah prophesied almost five hundred years before Christ and spoke of the people looking on the "one they have pierced" and being repentant. When people realize that the Messiah came and was put to death, it brings tremendous sorrow, but God has promised to turn it into joy and salvation.

> "And I will pour out on the house of David and the inhabitants of Jerusalem a spirit of grace and supplication. They will look on me, the one they have pierced, and they will mourn for him as one mourns for an only child, and grieve bitterly for him as one grieves for a firstborn son." (Zechariah 12:10)

This also highlights an important point about the Jewish people. God's promises and love for Jerusalem and Israel have not changed. Though He loves all nations, there are promises He has made about this land that have come to pass in modern times and will continue to be fulfilled. As the apostle Paul wrote to the Romans:

> I do not want you to be ignorant of this mystery, brothers and sisters, so that you may not be conceited: Israel has experienced a hardening in part until the full number of the Gentiles has come in, and in this way all Israel will be saved. As it is written:

"The deliverer will come from Zion;

> he will turn godlessness away from Jacob.

And this is my covenant with them

> when I take away their sins." (Romans 11:25–27)

God's love for Israel and the Jewish people is unchangeable.

4. The Government Will Be on His Shoulders

The prophet Isaiah foretold the fact that God would come into the world in the form of a child. This is indeed a great mystery that the infinite Creator would enter His own creation in this fashion. This was no ordinary child. Charles Spurgeon wrote, "Jesus Christ, even he who lay in Bethlehem's manger . . . [was] 'upholding all things by the word of His power.'"[10]

For to us a child is born,

> to us a son is given,

> > and the government will be on his shoulders.

And he will be called

> Wonderful Counselor, Mighty God,

> Everlasting Father, Prince of Peace.

Of the greatness of his government and peace

> there will be no end. (Isaiah 9:6–7)

The book of Isaiah is filled with references to the Messiah and the promise of peace and deliverance as a result of His work. This passage tells that the government will be on His shoulders. This means that regardless of who the earthly rulers and kings are, there is a greater King who rules. He, in fact, is called King of kings and Lord of lords! It also states that this child will be called Mighty God. There is no human who would dare take that title upon himself. But Jesus would be called *Immanuel*, meaning "God is with us." Though His rule started small (just twelve followers), it has continued to increase and bring peace to the lives of people and nations that have followed His Words.

5. Messiah's Timetable

Another startling prediction was the very time in history when the Messiah would appear. Daniel had been reading Jeremiah and saw that the predicted captivity of seventy years was coming to an end. After Daniel sought the Lord in prayer and fasting, the angel Gabriel came to him with this message describing future events, particularly the coming of the Messiah (Anointed One).

> "Know and understand this: From the time the word goes out to restore and rebuild Jerusalem until the Anointed One, the ruler, comes, there will be seven 'sevens,' and sixty-two 'sevens.' It will be rebuilt with streets and a trench, but in times of trouble. After the sixty-two 'sevens,' the Anointed One will be put to death and will have nothing. The people of the ruler who will come will destroy the city and the sanctuary. The end will come like a flood: War will continue until the end, and desolations have been decreed. He will confirm a covenant with many for one 'seven.' In the middle of the 'seven' he will put an end to sacrifice and offering. And at the temple he will set up an abomination that causes desolation, until the end that is decreed is poured out on him." (Daniel 9:25–27)

Daniel was told that the number of years between the decree to rebuild Jerusalem and the time the Anointed One would be "cut off" would be sixty-nine "sevens" or sixty-nine sets of seven years (483 years), which is at the time of Jesus' crucifixion in AD 30.[11] The book of Daniel also gives a startling picture of the work that He would accomplish. "Seventy 'sevens' are decreed for your people and your holy city to finish transgression, to put an end to sin, to atone for wickedness, to bring in everlasting righteousness, to seal up vision and prophecy and to anoint the Most Holy Place" (Daniel 9:24).

The Messiah would put an end to sin, atone for wickedness, and bring in everlasting righteousness. This glorious prophecy of the work of Christ was not only foretold then, but it is also available now to all who believe in Jesus, more than two thousand years later.

6. The Son of Man

Jesus frequently referred to Himself as the "Son of Man."

Jesus replied, "Foxes have dens and birds of the air have nests, but the Son of Man has no place to lay his head."
—Matthew 8:20

"When you are persecuted in one place, flee to another. Truly I tell you, you will not finish going through the towns of Israel before the Son of Man comes."
—Matthew 10:23

"Whoever is ashamed of me and my words, the Son of Man will be ashamed of them when he comes in his glory and in the glory of the Father and of the holy angels."
—Luke 9:26

These references are not just intended to call attention to His humanity, but they are a direct connection to the prophetic vision seen by Daniel almost five hundred years before Christ:

"In my vision at night I looked, and there before me was one like a son of man, coming with the clouds of heaven. He approached the Ancient of Days and was led into his presence. He was given authority, glory and sovereign power; all nations and peoples of every language worshiped him. His dominion is an everlasting dominion that will not pass away, and his kingdom is one that will never be destroyed." (Daniel 7:13–14)

There is no way that a mere man would be given this kind of descriptive title and told that all nations would worship Him. Jesus fulfilled this vision during His earthly ministry when He allowed people to worship Him. This act is a clear indication of His divine identity. Dr William Lane Craig agrees: "Jesus did not refer to Himself as 'a son of man,' but as 'the Son of Man.' Jesus' use of the phrase with the definite article 'the' is consistent throughout the gospels. By using the definite article, Jesus was directing attention to the divine-human figure prophesied in Daniel 7:13–14."[12]

7. The Son of God

There is no verse in the Bible more familiar to multitudes around the world than John 3:16. It is seen on billboards, painted on the faces of athletes, and quoted to those who are wanting to know the way of salvation. It reads, "For God so loved the world that he gave his one and only Son, that whoever believes in him shall not perish but have eternal life." Next to the term *Christ*, which means "Messiah," the title of the Son of God as used in John also points to the divinity of Jesus and links Him to being the Messiah. The second psalm gives the prophetic picture of this identity:

> Why do the nations conspire
>> and the peoples plot in vain?
> The kings of the earth rise up
>> and the rulers band together
>> against the LORD and against his anointed, saying,
> "Let us break their chains
>> and throw off their shackles."

> The One enthroned in heaven laughs;
>> the Lord scoffs at them.
> He rebukes them in his anger
>> and terrifies them in his wrath, saying,
> "I have installed my king
>> on Zion, my holy mountain."
> I will proclaim the LORD's decree:

> He said to me, "You are my son;
>> today I have become your father.
> Ask me,
>> and I will make the nations your inheritance,
>> the ends of the earth your possession.
> You will break them with a rod of iron;
>> you will dash them to pieces like pottery."

> Therefore, you kings, be wise;
>> be warned, you rulers of the earth.
> Serve the LORD with fear
>> and celebrate his rule with trembling.
> Kiss his son, or he will be angry
>> and your way will lead to your destruction,
> for his wrath can flare up in a moment.
>> Blessed are all who take refuge in him. (Psalm 2:1–12)

The concept of God having a Son is difficult to grasp. The expression does not mean that God had a child in the same way people procreate. By examining the Scriptures and trusting the Holy Spirit's illumination, the true meaning becomes clear. God became man in Jesus Christ. By entering the earth as a child, He was purposely taking on our humanity in order to save us. He also modeled the relationship God desires between us as His adopted sons and daughters. The apostle Paul explained His act of humility to the Philippian church:

> In your relationships with one another, have the same mindset
> as Christ Jesus:
>
> Who, being in very nature God,
>> did not consider equality with God something to be used
>>> to his own advantage,
> rather, he made himself nothing
>> by taking the very nature of a servant,
>> being made in human likeness.
> And being found in appearance as a man,
>> he humbled himself

by becoming obedient to death—
even death on a cross!

Therefore God exalted him to the highest place
and gave him the name that is above every name,
that at the name of Jesus every knee should bow,
in heaven and on earth and under the earth,
and every tongue acknowledge that Jesus Christ is Lord,
to the glory of God the Father. (Philippians 2:5–11)

THE DEITY OF CHRIST

Jesus was not only the promised Messiah, but He was the Creator of the universe, in human form. This claim is the greatest stumbling block that prevents the Jewish people from accepting *Yeshua* as the promised Savior. The picture of Jesus as Messiah has been clearly set forth in this book. Now we look deeper into the truth that Jesus was indeed God in the flesh.

As we have discussed, the words and the works of Jesus are beyond that of simply an exalted prophet or teacher. He made statements beyond just speaking for God and spoke as God Himself. There are also direct statements made by Jesus that reveal His identity as God.

In the beginning was the Word, and the Word was with God, and the Word was God. He was in the beginning with God. All things were made through Him, and without Him nothing was made that was made.

And the Word became flesh and dwelt among us, and

we beheld His glory, the glory as of the only begotten of the Father, full of grace and truth.

John bore witness of Him and cried out, saying, "This was He of whom I said, 'He who comes after me is preferred before me, for He was before me.'"

And of His fullness we have all received, and grace for grace. For the law was given through Moses, but grace and truth came through Jesus Christ. No one has seen God at any time. The only begotten Son, who is in the bosom of the Father, He has declared Him. (John 1:1–3, 14–18 NKJV)

These verses tell us that the Word was God and that the Word became flesh and lived among us. The Word is personified with the pronoun "Him" and states, "without Him [the Word] nothing was made that was made." This revelation that Christ was indeed the Creator was expressed by the apostle Paul:

The Son [Jesus] is the image of the invisible God, the firstborn over all creation. For in him all things were created: things in heaven and on earth, visible and invisible, whether thrones or powers or rulers or authorities; all things have been created through him and for him. He is before all things, and in him all things hold together. (Colossians 1:15–17)

It was this very truth that ultimately caused the religious authorities to press to have Jesus crucified. His statements that pointed to His divinity were considered blasphemous and, therefore, worthy of death. None was more incriminating than Jesus using the title that God had used when He revealed Himself to Moses: I AM.

"Your father Abraham rejoiced at the thought of seeing my day; he saw it and was glad."

"You are not yet fifty years old," they said to him, "and you have seen Abraham!"

"Very truly I tell you," Jesus answered, "before Abraham was born, I am!" At this, they picked up stones to stone him, but Jesus hid himself, slipping away from the temple grounds. (John 8:56–59)

These passages explicitly point to Jesus Christ as God. The other gospels identify Jesus as God more implicitly by applying Old Testament passages that reference God to Him. For instance, John the Baptist prepared Jesus' way while the Old Testament describes him as preparing the way for God (Malachi 4:5–6). Likewise, Jesus described Himself as the Good Shepherd who would gather His sheep (John 10:14–16) while the Old Testament uses the same description for God (Jeremiah 23:3).[13] This mystery has been given the theological name of the Trinity. In essence, there is one God, in three persons: Father, Son, and Holy Spirit. All three are given the honor and reverence as God. The ancient creeds from Nicea and Chalcedon give the outworking of the theological language that is used to express the many dimensions of this truth.

In the end the Trinity is a mystery that Scripture reveals. It is not irrational as much as it is super-rational or trans-rational. When dealing with an uncreated, all-knowing God, we should accept from the start that God is not like us (although we bear His likeness in various ways). The fact that the evidence points to an uncreated being should humble us from the outset to accept what God says as true even if we do not fully understand it.

Jesus Is Lord

Calling on the name of the Lord is the greatest privilege and opportunity humankind has ever been given. The title "Lord" needs to be understood and shown to mean God Himself, not the mere title given to men, such as "Lord Churchill." This distinction is essential since to be saved, we must believe that Jesus is Lord.

> If you declare with your mouth, "Jesus is Lord," and believe in your heart that God raised him from the dead, you will be saved. For it is with your heart that you believe and are justified, and it is with your mouth that you profess your faith and are saved. As Scripture says, "Anyone who believes in him will never be put to shame." For there is no difference between Jew and Gentile—the same Lord is Lord of all and richly blesses all who call on him, for, "Everyone who calls on the name of the Lord will be saved." (Romans 10:9–13)

The title Lord in Greek is the same word in Hebrew used for *God*, as seen in several New Testament passages. Paul attributes to Jesus the title Lord (*kyrios*) in his letters (e.g., Romans 10:9, 13), and he directly associates that title with God in his quotations of Old Testament passages (e.g., Romans 9:27–28). Also, the earliest prayer of the Christian community was the Aramaic phrase *Maranatha*, which translates "the (our) Lord come." Since the phrase is in Aramaic, it must have originated with the early Palestinian Christians during Jesus' ministry. The word *mar* has the same meaning as *kyrios*, and it is used in Old Testament passages to refer to God. The expression is also used in the *Didache*, which is a collection of the apostles' teachings, dating to the late first century. Paul uses it in one of his letters to the Corinthians (1 Corinthians 16:22), where it appears shortly after the early creedal formula in 1 Corinthians 15. This creed describes Jesus' death as paying for people's sins, which further reflects His divine nature. These descriptions originated very soon after the resurrection, which completely refutes the claim that the belief in Jesus' divine nature developed over time.

SUMMARY

Beyond the specific stories of Jesus and the prophetic announce-ments that heralded His advent, there is a grand illustrative portrait of Christ the Redeemer that is painted in the very fabric of every book in the Bible, not just the Gospels. I remember hear-ing a legendary preacher walk through every book in the Bible from memory and showed how the whole of Scripture spoke of Jesus Christ. He said, "Christ is seen in Exodus as the Passover lamb, in Numbers as the pillar of cloud by day and fire by night. In Joshua, He was the captain of our salvation; in Judges, he's our lawgiver."[14] He went on to conclude that in Revelation "he is Lord of lords and King of kings" (Revelation 17:14).

Author David Limbaugh expounds on the words Jesus spoke after His resurrection to two of His disciples as they walked along the roughly seven-mile journey from Jerusalem to the vil-lage of Emmaus. In response to the reports of His own tomb being empty, Jesus replied, "'How foolish you are, and how slow to believe all that the prophets have spoken! Did not the Messiah have to suffer these things and then enter his glory?'

And beginning with Moses and all the Prophets, he explained to them what was said in all the Scriptures concerning himself" (Luke 24:25-27).

> Jesus illuminates Scripture for the two men on the Emmaus road and does the same for His disciples. The New Testament is strikingly clear that He affirms the Old Testament is all about Him. Therefore, if we believe in Him and that all Scripture is God–breathed, as it professes to be, we too must accept that its singular focus is on our Savior. Once you acknowledge that, your understanding and reverence for the Bible will greatly increase.[15]

By showing Christ revealed in every book, there is no doubt that Jesus is indeed the living God in human form. When He is given the honor and preeminence He deserves, then we come into true freedom, not bondage. By understanding and fully embracing the deity of Jesus Christ, we can be transformed from self-centered creatures into sons and daughters of the God of the universe.

8

MIRACLES

Evidence of the Supernatural

Western theology invariably asks the question:
Are miracles possible? This of course addresses the
Enlightenment problem of a closed universe. In much of
Asia that is a non-question because the miraculous
is assumed and fairly regularly experienced.[1]
—HWA YUNG (BISHOP EMERITUS OF MALAYSIA)

THE REALITY THAT JESUS IS LORD, THE PROMISED Messiah, had a powerful and practical effect on the world. From the beginning the apostles preached the gospel and demonstrated God's stamp of approval by showing the authority of the name of Jesus. They explained that the healings and miracles that followed their preaching were not because of any special power of their own but through faith in Jesus' name. "By faith in the name of Jesus, this man whom you see and know was made strong. It is Jesus' name and the faith that comes through him that has completely healed him, as you can all see" (Acts 3:16).

That same faith in His name can still produce the kind of results today that it did two thousand years ago. This is the truth that compelled me after my college graduation to devote my life to reaching the world for Christ. The reality that *all things are possible to him who believes* caused me to wake up every day with a sense of expectation of good things that could happen, regardless of how bleak and desperate the circumstance. This included the Holy Spirit's guidance when it came to sharing my faith with others.

My journey as a minister, in fact, started with a supernatural encounter. Funny enough, it did not take place in a church. While I was playing a game of pickup basketball at Mississippi State University, the Holy Spirit impressed on my mind a message about a young man playing on another court in the gym. Though I heard no voice, there was a distinct sense that God was speaking to me about him: *he's been praying for someone to talk to him about Me.* It seemed apparent to me that this was a message I was to tell him. This experience reminds me of a scene from the movie, *It's a Wonderful Life*, when Clarence the Angel tells George Bailey (Jimmy Stewart) that he's been sent as an answer to his prayer. He responds, "You look like the kind of angel I'd get." This young man on the court was a big, intimidating guy, and I had a little apprehension that neither the message nor me as the messenger would be perceived as the answer to his prayer. Was I in for a shock! When I finally mustered the courage to introduce myself to him, my approach was a little abrupt and awkward. I told him what I felt God had told me about him, and his jaw literally dropped. He had prayed that very prayer the night before.

In the next few days, he would fully commit his life to Christ, and several of his friends would follow his decision as well. That moment proved to be the beginning of a lifelong calling to reach university students. Throughout the years God has helped me in many supernatural ways through insights into people's lives as well as physical healings and other answers to prayers that were offered in the name of Jesus. Sometimes those answers came instantly; others were manifested over time.

The reports of healings and miracles happening around the world have caused dramatic growth in the Christian faith. As I traveled to other nations, I began to see and hear of God's power at work in phenomenal ways. In Korea, this once predominantly Buddhist nation, a spiritual awakening was taking place because of these kinds of demonstrations of God's power. I attended an outdoor meeting there in 1984, with more than one million in attendance. The same pattern can be seen in China.

In China the growth of Christianity was taking place because the supernatural accompanied the preaching of the gospel. The China Christian Council estimated that "half of the new conversions of the last twenty years have been caused by faith healing experiences." Other researchers have suggested that recent figures could be as high as 90 percent.[2]

The evidence for miracles is too overwhelming to dismiss as coincidence. We have seen the same dramatic supernatural manifestations around the world on college campuses. This setting is important because students can certainly tend to be skeptical. If something happens that is inexplicable in terms of natural causes, they are reticent to ascribe it to being a miracle or a direct result of divine action.

Remember, to be a Christian means that you believe that Christ was miraculously raised from the dead, three days after

His death. If this was the only miracle that ever happened, it would still be enough to put our trust in Him. However, this foundational miracle points to the fact that all the other miracles recorded in the Gospels were real as well. Not only the dramatic physical miracles, but the supernatural leading and guidance of the Holy Spirit. As Jesus said to the apostles, "You will receive power when the Holy Spirit comes on you; and you will be my witnesses in Jerusalem, and in all Judea and Samaria, and to the ends of the earth" (Acts 1:8).

While our faith must be grounded fully in the work of Jesus Christ in His life, death, and resurrection, we must be open to His working in the lives of people today as well. There are indeed moments when the supernatural hand of God breaks into our lives and communities in such a way that it is an undeniable witness to His continuing presence and work in the world. In the face of overwhelming pain and suffering all around us, we have not been left without the hope of His providing help. Such experiences are why after thirty years of being a Christian I still believe that "with God nothing will be impossible" (Luke 1:37 NKJV).

Today most of humanity believes miracles are possible as well. To believe in God is to believe that He is able to alter circumstances, events, sickness, and impossible situations. Often even the atheist will pause to give God the chance to prove Himself by healing a loved one or friend. Many times the presence of unyielding pain and suffering convinces the skeptic that his unbelief is justified. But when these miraculous moments take place, they produce a faith in people that becomes unshakable. The goal of this chapter is to establish the philosophical *possibility* of miracles, as well as the biblical and historical testimony of their reality and the principles by which they work.

The Existence of God Is Evidence for the Supernatural

First of all, if God exists, then the supernatural dimension is real. The philosophy of naturalism asserts that nature is all there is. This notion has been thoroughly addressed in my book *God's Not Dead* and was referenced again in the introduction of this book.

The evidence for miracles is overwhelming. In order to dismiss the testimonials of supernatural events, you have to rule out ahead of time (a priori) the possibility of miracles. In other words, in order to believe no miracles have ever happened, one must begin by assuming no miracles can happen. This logic is circular reasoning and therefore self-defeating from the outset. In contrast, the argument for the possibility of miracles is logically plausible and could be stated in this way:

—There is evidence that an uncaused, nonmaterial Creator exists who is responsible for bringing nature into existence.
—This Creator (God) would be supernatural in nature and essence.
—This supernatural Creator could interact with our world and cause certain events to happen beyond what solely natural laws could produce.

This argument is supported by the many types of evidence that point to God's existence. From science, physicists have recognized for decades that the universe appeared to have a beginning. And the laws of physics seem to have been designed with life in mind. If gravity were ever so slightly larger or smaller, planets would not exist, which would make life impossible. Similarly, for life to exist on earth, countless details had to be set perfectly for our planet, sun, moon, and solar system. For instance, the earth needs to be the right distance from the sun, have the right rotation rate, and the proper atmosphere. From biology, the first cell on earth required DNA, which contains the instructions for its operations and reproduction. These instructions contain significant amounts of information, and information is only the product of an intelligent designer. All of these facts point to a creator outside of time and space who created our universe, planet, and life.[3]

One of the most common confusions about miracles is that believing in them means that one has to dismiss science. However, the fact that physical laws exist does not mean that the Creator of those laws is not able to intervene in His own creation. Some mistakenly dismiss miracles by misunderstanding what is taking place. They assume that a miracle is somehow a violation of the laws of nature, which they assume contradicts human experience. In reality, it is because we know the laws of nature that we are able to detect when something unusual or outside of those laws has happened. A professor of mathematics at Oxford University, John Lennox explains this important distinction:

> The second objection is that now that we know the laws of nature, miracles are impossible, but that involves a further fallacy. Suppose I put $1,000 tonight in my hotel room in Cambridge and I put $1,000 in tomorrow night. One plus one equals two; that's $2,000. On the third day, I opened the drawer and I find $500. Now, what do I say? Do I say the laws of arithmetic have been broken? Or the laws of the United States have been broken?[4]

As demonstrated, the arguments against the possibility of miracles are inherently flawed. The evidence falls into the categories of the evidence from scripture, from history, and from science.

The Testimony of Scripture

Jesus Christ is the same yesterday and today and forever.

—Hebrews 13:8

As we learned earlier, the gospel records are reliable accounts of the life and words of Jesus. However, skeptical New Testament scholars persist in dismissing any stories of Jesus healing the sick or casting out demons as unhistorical, primarily because of their prior disbelief in their possibility. However, the weight of evidence in the past few decades has forced even some of the most skeptical to acknowledge that the Gospels are accurate in their portrayal of Jesus as both a miracle worker and an exorcist.[5]

This shift resulted from the recognition that the miracle stories meet numerous minimal fact criteria. Foremost, they permeate every layer of the Gospels and the book of Acts. Several events, such as the miraculous feeding, are mentioned by all four Gospels. Some examples also meet the criteria of embarrassment, such as the disciples' inability to cast out a demon before Jesus arrives (Matthew 17:14–16, Mark 9:17–18). What Christian would make up stories that would make their respected leaders look so bad? Many accounts also meet the criteria of dissimilarity. Unlike all other healers and exorcists at that time, Jesus did not invoke any higher power to perform His healings and exorcisms but acted under His own authority. His miracles are also unique in their magnitude and frequency.[6] In addition, even the historian Josephus, who was not a Christian, described Jesus as a "doer of amazing deeds."[7] Such evidence even convinced arch-skeptic Marcus Borg to state that the facts are "virtually indisputable that Jesus was a healer and exorcist."[8]

Critics may accept the accounts at least to some extent as genuine, but they attempt to rationalize them away as misinterpretations of the actual events. In the end, they believe that all descriptions of Jesus' healing the sick or casting out evil powers have natural explanations. For instance, they often claim that people who appeared to be healed by Jesus might have simply convinced themselves that they were made better due to the power of suggestion. But such explanations are difficult to imagine given both the dramatic and instantaneous nature of the purported healings. How could someone, who had been paralyzed since birth, through the power of suggestion begin to walk?

Furthermore, as we established in an earlier chapter, the evidence for the resurrection itself is compelling. And if the resurrection took place, then the miraculous does not only become possible but probable. Therefore, the accounts of miracles from the New Testament must also be considered possible, which leads to the clear conclusion that they actually happened.

Miracles Throughout History

Even after the death of the first apostles, Christians continued to heal the sick through prayer and cast out evil powers as Jesus had done. These signs were recorded by numerous early church leaders. For instance, Irenaeus in the second century wrote about people being raised from the dead in the name of Jesus:

> [Heretics are] so far . . . from being able to raise the dead, as
> the Lord raised them and the apostles did by means of prayer,

and as has been frequently done in the brotherhood on account of some necessity. The entire church in that particular locality entreating with much fasting and prayer, the spirit of the dead man has returned, and he has been bestowed in answer to the prayers of the saints.[9]

Athanasius wrote in the fourth century about Christian miracle workers among the bishops and monks, "So take these as an example, beloved Dracontius, and do not say, or believe those who say, that the bishop's office is an occasion to sin. . . . For we know both bishops who fast and monks who eat. We know bishops who drink no wine as well as monks who do. We know bishops who work miracles as well as monks who do not."[10]

Several other church fathers also described miracles in their midst, including (to name just a few) Athanasius, Origen, Tertullian, and Chrysostom. Some, such as Augustine, were eyewitnesses of the events, and several used them apologetically to both defend the Christian faith and to challenge heretics. Other ancient writings described miracles as a primary motivation in the conversion of Jews and pagans. Even enemies of the Christians acknowledged the miraculous power they demonstrated. The commonality of miracles varied throughout church history, but the consistent and authoritative testimony to their existence is undeniable.

In his book *Miracles: The Credibility of the New Testament Accounts*, Craig Keener documented historical records of miracles throughout history in all parts of the world. Some of the most dramatic stories have taken place in the last century. For instance, several healing ministers in the early twentieth century reported thousands of cases of miraculous healings, including instantaneous recovery from cancer, broken bones, blindness, and countless other maladies. Several cases have even been medically documented.

Keener has also collected stories of miracles occurring in many parts of the world today. The statistics of their frequency in many regions are gripping. A 2006 Pew Forum survey was conducted on experiencing the miraculous in ten countries. The results indicated that the number of Christians who experienced a miracle was roughly two hundred million. And I haven't even mentioned the thousands of Muslims in the Middle East, converting to Christianity after experiencing Jesus Christ in a dream. Many of the dream descriptions were the same even though the recipients had never met.

"Against Miracles"—Responding to Hume

As mentioned earlier, many scientists and philosophers immediately dismiss the miracle stories because they deny the existence of anything beyond nature. They often justify their position by appealing to the arguments made by eighteenth-century philosopher David Hume against the existence of miracles. To give a condensed version of Hume's argument, he begins by claiming that everyone's everyday experiences indicate that all events are governed by natural laws. This experience is so uniform that any claim that something occurred that seems to violate those laws (i.e., is miraculous) must be taken with the highest skepticism. He also argues that witnesses to miracles are illiterate, uneducated, and superstitious, so their testimony cannot be trusted. Therefore, any natural explanation for the event, no matter how improbable, should be preferred to believing in a miracle, which is effectively impossible.

The problem with Hume's argument is, as many philosophers have noted, his use of circular reasoning. He assumes from the beginning that the everyday experience of all people is that the laws of nature alone dictate all that happens. And the only testimony of events that seem to violate those laws comes from people who are superstitious and uneducated. For if they were trustworthy, they would never have claimed to have witnessed something miraculous, which is clearly impossible. He then concludes that miracles do not happen due to a lack of "reliable" evidence. To summarize, Hume throws out all evidence for the miraculous by assuming any such evidence could only come from people who are unreliable, for only unreliable people would claim something that is impossible. To condense even more, he argues that miracles do not occur, because he knows miracles do not occur.

A similar critique of Hume is given by William Lane Craig, who summarizes philosopher Gottfried Less:

> Hume's principal argument is that testimony to miracles has the experience of the world and the centuries against it. In response, Less argues: (1) Because nature is the freely willed order of God, a miracle is just as possible as any event. Therefore, it is just as believable as any event. (2) Testimony to an event cannot be refuted by experiences and observations. Otherwise we would never be justified in believing anything outside our present experience; no new discoveries would be possible. (3) There is no contradiction between experience and Christian miracles. Miracles are different events (*contraria*) from experience in general, but not contradictory events (*contradictoria*) to experience in general.[11]

As with the resurrection, if one does not deny God's existence from the beginning, the existence of miracles is not only possible but to be expected. A second problem with Hume's argument also relates to his use of evidence. He set extraordinarily high standards in evaluating claims of miracles. However, people in his day presented him with cases that met his criteria. In response, he simply added new criteria or proposed fantastically improbable alternatives. He responded to the evidence similarly to the manner in which skeptics respond today, through denial and blind faith in naturalistic philosophy. As Keener comments:

> Hume presupposes a standard of proof so high that any evidence is effectively ruled out in advance. That is, Hume so frames his position that he renders it unfalsifiable—and therefore not tenable for public discourses by traditional standards of logic. Unfortunately, this heads-I-win, tails-you-lose form of argument remains popular even today, even with respect to miracles. For example, roughly two decades ago I asked one professor, who was dismissing evidence for miracles, if he would believe in supernatural activity if someone were raised from the dead in front of him. He responded, consistent to his approach, that he would not. Interestingly, some doubt that even Hume, being an empiricist, would have insisted that the person was not raised from the dead if he himself witnessed it.[12]

Hume's assumption that people do not regularly experience the miraculous only applied to his cultural context. Moreover, many miracle cases meet Hume's most exacting criteria in the quality of their scientific documentation.

Scientific Evidence for Miracles

Many of the miracles around the world today are experienced in areas with little access to the equipment and trained medical personnel needed for proper scientific documentation. God demonstrates His power most often among people with the least exposure to Christian teaching, which at least at the moment happens to correspond to regions least influenced by globalization. However, some medical professionals have taken the time to collect proper records. Keener includes several references to cases where doctors have extensive documentation, including pre- and post-healing X-rays or CAT-scans.

Skeptics often argue that such data are not entirely convincing since some serious illnesses occasionally go into remission spontaneously. However, some of the recorded cases include complete recoveries occurring immediately after prayer, and a large collection of the healings resulted from the ministry of a single person, such as Kathryn Kuhlman. The chances are fantastically small that a single person would pray for numerous people and see such a high proportion of them have extremely unlikely spontaneous recoveries. The only reasonable explanation in these examples is genuine supernatural interventions.

A group of Christian scholars even published an article on healing resulting from the ministry of Heidi Baker. The study documented the impact of a healing crusade, where Dr. Baker and colleagues extensively prayed for the recovery of hearing and vision. The researchers tested the hearing and vision of attendees before and after prayer. The hearing and the vision improved so much in so many participants that the differences could not be explained by anything other than God answering prayer.[13]

WHY IS NOT EVERYONE HEALED?

As mentioned, the number of people claiming to have had specific prayers answered are in the hundreds of millions. On a typical Sunday in our church with hundreds of members, I will ask for a show of hands as to how many present know beyond a shadow of a doubt that they have had a specific prayer answered. Almost all the people present raise their hands. Skeptics immediately assume their experiences were merely coincidences that are attributed to God. But to those who experienced them, they are real. And much historical and scientific documentation exists to suggest many are correct.

Yet a challenging question still remains. Why do so many prayers, particularly for healings, seem to go unanswered? Remember, the focus of this book is on the evidence for the historical Jesus of the Gospels. Our faith is in Jesus Christ and His death, burial, and resurrection. Those events are true regardless of whether my latest petition to God was answered or not. However, the question still weighs heavily on many Christians' hearts.

One of the atheist websites asks the question a bit differently: "Why doesn't God heal amputees?" This question is phrased as if it is the ultimate argument that God does not exist and therefore cannot respond to prayers. The answer to this apparent quandary is straightforward: How do you know He hasn't? Just because you have never seen it, does not mean it has not happened.

I have spoken to people who witnessed firsthand miracle stories in places like India and throughout Africa. They claim to have seen limbs restored, empty eye sockets receiving sight, and even the dead raised back to life. Immediately, skeptics chide that they refuse to believe such stories. But their lack of belief does not mean these miracles did not happen. This type of attitude was addressed in the book of Acts, after many notable miracles had taken place and the cities were being stirred by these reports:

Take care that what the prophets have said does not happen to you:

"'Look, you scoffers,
wonder and perish,
for I am going to do something in your days
that you would never believe
even if someone told you.'" (Acts 13:40–41)

The real question skeptics are asking is, "Why doesn't God just heal everyone, everywhere, on demand?" Even more they are asking, "Why is there pain and suffering at all?"

In particular, answers to prayer, such as divine healings, are signs of God's ultimate redemption of creation, which point to the truth of Jesus (John 20:30–31), but the full restoration will come only at the end of history when Jesus returns. We now live in a fallen world, so even the most devout of believers will experience pain, suffering, and disease. However, we know that God will eventually make all things right. For the moment, God does not heal every sick person. That day will certainly come when Christ returns and we are standing fully in His presence. For now, He presents enough signs to convince people who truly desire to know the truth yet not so many signs as to force people into believing if they have no desire to do so. As the seventeenth-century mathematician and philosopher Blaise Pascal said, "He has given signs of Himself, visible to those who seek Him, and not to those who seek Him not. There is enough light for those who only desire to see, and enough obscurity for those who have a contrary disposition."[14]

Today Christians can rejoice for those who experience healings and extraordinary answers to prayer, but we can also endure trials and suffering, knowing that one day God will remove all evil and suffering from the world and resurrect us to spend eternity in His presence.

MODERN-DAY MIRACLES

Around the world the stories of healings and other miracles are as abundant as they are astounding. Many books have chronicled testimonies of these occurrences and provided firsthand verification. However, regardless of the amount of evidence and personal testimony provided, room always exists for the skeptical mind to dismiss reports of this nature. Yet the experiences described not only convinced the recipients that they were genuine, but many met the most rigorous requirements of scientific investigation. Here are a few examples.

Healings and Miracles

Countless cases of extraordinary miracles have been documented by historians, researchers, and medical professionals. The following are but a small sample that Craig Keener and others have collected. The first case centers on a boy named Onel in

Placetas, Villa Clara, Cuba, who had malformed bones in his feet. An X-ray showed that the lower bones were becoming like sand. He was expected to lose his ability to walk in about a year. Onel was prayed for by visiting evangelist Otto De La Torre. The feet were X-rayed later in the week and the new X-ray showed that they were now completely normal. The doctor was originally convinced the X-rays were mixed up, but he later confirmed his diagnosis was correct. Onel's family still has the before and after X-rays.[15]

Elaine Panelo from the Philippines contracted liver cancer and went to a local hospital for help. Her doctors determined that her cancer was too advanced for medical treatment. Her condition continued to deteriorate, and she eventually died. She was then taken to the morgue. A Baptist pastor decided to pray for her, even though she was not sure if she believed in divine healing. Elaine's head started moving, and she came fully back to life. The symptoms of her cancer seemed to have subsided. She eventually went back to one of her original doctors, who refused to believe she was the same person. After she checked the original records, the dramatic nature of the healing convinced her and her husband to become Christians.[16]

A final example is one of many miracle accounts researched by Dr. Richard Casdorph, which he documents with X-ray photos in his book *The Miracles*.[17] Marion had been diagnosed with multiple sclerosis, and her condition deteriorated steadily until she was not even able to eat. She also developed a deformed forearm. She went to a healing meeting, where she felt that she had been healed. In particular, she found herself able to stand and walk for the first time in years. A doctor later confirmed that she had been completely healed, including the deformed arm. She and her husband then became believers.[18]

Near Death Experiences

Another category of evidence that supports the existence of the supernatural, is near death experiences (NDE). Thousands of people claimed to have remained conscious after entering a state on the threshold of death. Many report visiting an afterlife environment, where they encounter deceased relatives and supernatural beings. In some cases, patients' brain activity ceased, yet the patients were able to remember vivid details of events in their surroundings. For some, the details are so numerous and so specific that the only possible explanation is that the patients' consciousness left their bodies.

One of the more dramatic cases involved a thirty-five-year-old woman. During her surgery, it was determined that an extraordinary secondary medical procedure nicknamed "standstill" was necessary. The blood was drained from her head, her body was cooled down to sixty degrees, her heart was purposely stopped, and her brain waves totally flattened. Cardiologist Michael Sabom attests that her brain was dead, as indicated by three different medical tests—a silent EEG, no brain-stem response, and an absence of blood in the brain. She was in this later state for more than an hour. After surgery she reported an amazing array of details regarding about a half-dozen points, including both occurrences and their timing, that were later corroborated from the medical records kept during the operation. Then she claimed to have visited a heavenly location where she had discussions with several deceased relatives. On an NDE scale developed by University of Virginia psychiatrist Bruce Greyson, she scored what Sabom termed "an amazing depth" of NDE.[19]

My Personal Experience

There have been numerous times that I have witnessed an act of supernatural healing or an answer to prayer that was undeniably a result of God's intervention. I've seen blind people see and deaf people hear after prayer. I have watched as people who were lame or incapacitated begin to walk as well. The most common experience is to see people recover from an illness or an accident after doctors have given up hope. Even some of my own family members have recovered miraculously from serious illnesses.

At the same time, there are just as many cases, if not more, where there was no healing or miracle. Numerous times when I or others prayed, the person was not healed and passed away. Those moments cause one to pull back and feel tempted to stop praying for others in order to avoid the disappointment of not seeing a prayer answered. At such times, I remind myself that my job is not to heal anyone or to second-guess why situations do not always work out the way I desired. The real failure is not to pray in the first place. Usually nothing happens if we do nothing.

I am convinced that it is never too late to come to know Christ as Healer and Deliverer. All it takes is a little faith, the size of a small seed, and mountains will move. Each person has been given that measure of faith. The more we step out in faith, the more we will see it grow.

Without question, the greatest miracle happens when a person puts his or her trust in Christ and is born again and transferred out of the kingdom of darkness into the kingdom of God. It is my experience that all the other supernatural phenomena and signs God performs are ultimately intended to bring about this kind of change of heart.

LIVING BY FAITH

Before leaving this subject, I need to offer some practical thoughts on how to handle this powerful idea of the reality of a God who works miracles today and the balance of how we should then live on a day-to-day basis. As real as miracles may be, we are not called to live by miracles but to live by faith.

This means that we live in the tension of believing in miracles but not basing our lives on whether they happen when we want them to happen. In fact, to live by faith means that we trust God and His truth regardless of our circumstances. Faith is believing in God because of the overwhelming objective evidence He has already given, not the subjective experiences of what has happened to us lately. "For in the gospel the righteousness of God is revealed—a righteousness that is by faith from first to last, just as it is written: 'The righteous will live by faith'" (Romans 1:17).

Many maintain the mistaken notion that to have faith means to live in this constant flow of one miracle after another. As soon as trouble or tragedy comes into our lives, we conclude that God has abandoned us or we have done something wrong. I draw enormous comfort from the fact that the great men and women of faith in Scripture had to face times when it seemed that God was nowhere around. They served God faithfully regardless of their circumstances. The apostle Paul knew this all too well. Even though he had seen Jesus and performed multiple miracles, Paul suffered severely because of his faith. When he penned that inspirational verse, "I can do all things through Christ who strengthens me" (Philippians 4:13 NKJV), he was actually in prison with a chain around his leg.

As you move forward in the life of faith, it is vital to stay focused on Christ and His Word. If you look around at all of the volatile, uncertain circumstances, you can tend to feel overwhelmed. At such times, remember the apostle Peter when he stepped out of the boat to attempt to walk on water. He began to sink when he focused on the wind and the waves, but he recovered when he reached out for Jesus' hand. The secret to not being tossed like the surf of the sea is to determine to live your life by the principles of Scripture and keep your eyes on Jesus.

"Therefore, since we are surrounded by such a great cloud of witnesses, let us throw off everything that hinders and the sin that so easily entangles. And let us run with perseverance the race marked out for us, fixing our eyes on Jesus, the pioneer and perfecter of faith (Hebrews 12:1–2).

SUMMARY

The central thesis of this chapter is that because God is real, miracles are real.

The existence of a supernatural Creator means that the supernatural dimension exists, and thus the possibility of miracles exists as well. This reality became most clear when God became man in Jesus Christ and exhibited authority over disease, demons, and the environment. He then rose from the dead, which verified His identity as the Son of God and gave ultimate proof that a supernatural event had occurred.

We are called as believers to preach the good news of this resurrection from the dead and the hope that comes from the knowledge of the existence of God. We also remind believers that God cares about us and the world we live in, and He has promised to act on our behalf as we pray and reach out to others in His wonderful name. In the final two chapters we look at practically learning to follow Jesus, growing in our faith, and being able to reach out to others effectively and confidently. There's not a minute to waste.

9

FOLLOWING JESUS

Answering the Call to Discipleship

Discipleship is relationship, first with
God then with one another.[1]
—JOEY BONIFACIO

WE LIVE IN A BROKEN WORLD. REGARDLESS OF WHERE you live, your age or ethnic background, the pain of life is enormous. Currently, there are more than a hundred armed conflicts in the world.[2] Viruses such as Ebola threaten to sweep the world. (In 1918, more died because of the flu epidemic than did in World War I.) From what some call a looming economic Armageddon to a real one of biblical proportions, this tiny blue dot we call home has never been more vulnerable to self-destruction.

But without question, the most ominous and disturbing threat we currently face is terrorism. If you are a follower of Christ, you are often one of the most likely to be the target of this kind of intentional violence. The images we see on a regular basis are haunting. Men dressed in orange prison fatigues kneeling on a beach as masked members of ISIS prepare to sever their heads from their bodies. Coerced messages of ransom request filmed on cell phones. Often the reason is clearly spelled out—these are Christians, infidels according to these radical Muslims and their interpretation of the Koran.

The courage of these believers who are being martyred for their faith is deeply challenging and inspiring. Centuries ago, it was the same type of faith that the early Christians had to demonstrate in the face of Roman persecution.

In the early second century, Polycarp, a Christian leader who was trained by the apostle John, was offered freedom from prison and death in exchange for renouncing his faith in Christ. In response, he said, "Christ has been faithful to me—how could I not be faithful to Him?"[3] I often wonder what I would say in such a situation. I pray that I would be just as strong. These stirring examples remind us that faith in Christ compels us to hold to our testimony, even in the face of persecution or death. In fact, thousands of people lose their lives simply because they believe in Jesus Christ.

On the other hand, the roles should never be reversed. Under no circumstances should anyone ever be forced or coerced into believing in Jesus Christ. Looking back through history during the times of the Crusades and the Inquisition, when violence has been committed in the name of Jesus, it has been a result of disobeying Jesus' central command to "love your enemies" (Matthew 5:44).

Believing in Jesus is a call to follow His teachings of obedience to the law of love that He commanded, not just mental assent to a set of facts or propositions about Him. Very few will ever face this kind of opposition to their beliefs. For most of us, the resistance comes from social pressure or personal desires to conform to a lifestyle that is contradictory to the path Christ calls us to walk.

Over the centuries whenever the church lost its effectiveness and credibility, it compromised and strayed from the truth. "You are the salt of the earth. But if the salt loses its saltiness, how can it be made salty again? It is no longer good for anything, except to be thrown out and trampled underfoot" (Matthew 5:13). This scripture speaks of the Christian's role in acting as a preservative to the world around us. When we lose our salt we, in effect, become a nonfactor in helping anyone.

Today the predominant message you hear is centered on the word *grace*. In America this word has often been reduced to a tame affirmation that God loves you regardless of what you do or how you live. Though the grace of God is at the heart of our faith, it is far greater than many of us have imagined. It's the kind that gives you the burning desire to live a holy life and the power to do so. It forgives the vilest crime and transforms the darkest heart. As Paul wrote to the Romans, "For sin shall no longer be your master, because you are not under the law, but under grace" (Romans 6:14).

As an example, consider the courageous faith of William Wilberforce. The slave trade was abolished in England in 1833 largely because of his persistent efforts. A member of Parliament and a sincere Christian, Wilberforce labored for more than thirty years to see this pernicious evil end in all the British Empire. He used the force of Scripture to weigh on the minds and hearts of the leaders of the government until this wrong was righted. In his book *Real Christianity*, Bob Beltz spells out the shallowness and emptiness of this kind of incomplete grace.

This is a problem that doesn't afflict cultural Christians who do not possess what I have called authentic faith. This is a problem that is particularly problematic for those who legitimately have received Christ and believe all that the Bible teaches. Their belief system is intact, but their lives do not bear the evidence that they have actually had a real encounter with Christ. They regard their faith as something that has been taken care of and then proceed to live as if Christ were not really their Lord. True Christian grace has become cheap grace.[4]

Real grace is indeed unmerited favor from God. He forgives us and cleanses us from sin, regardless of how spiritually destitute and bleak our lives may be. But He doesn't leave us in this condition. The grace of God transforms and becomes an inner motivation to obey God's commands. "For the grace of God has appeared that offers salvation to all people. It teaches us to say 'No' to ungodliness and worldly passions, and to live self-controlled, upright and godly lives in this present age" (Titus 2:11–12). This kind of complete and true grace is marked by two distinct traits:

- *Radical love for God*
  Loving the Lord with all your heart, soul, and strength. This is what I remember about the people I met when I came to a belief in Christ. They loved the Lord with all their hearts. This was practically expressed in a love for God's word in Scripture as well as worship. To really love God means to love what He loves and hate what He hates. God hates sin, plain and simple. He hates it because it destroys people.

- *Radical love for others*

    You can't love God and not love others. This was what I saw in the people I met in college who were truly following Jesus. Not only did they have a passion for God, but they had a deep compassion for others as well. What struck me was how nonjudgmental and caring these people were. They didn't look down on others for not having the same faith and love for God; they simply demonstrated how real their faith was and made people want to experience that kind of love as well. Their love was relentless.

THE COST OF DISCIPLESHIP

This leads us to the questions of why so many people who claim to be Christian seem to lack this kind of life. After all, surveys show that one of the top reasons people dismiss the claims of Christ is because of the hypocrisy of those who profess the faith. This was certainly a big factor for me. After looking deeply into the Scriptures, as well as watching the lives of those who seem to come and go from church, I find one clear reason for this that stands out above all others: the absence of a commitment to surrender everything to the authority and lordship of Christ. This doesn't mean we have to be perfect and attempt to earn our way to heaven by our good works; it is, instead, a heart attitude of submission to the will of God and the truth of His Word. Jesus told a parable about the response someone has when he truly understands the value of this kind of relationship with God:

"The kingdom of heaven is like treasure hidden in a field. When a man found it, he hid it again, and then in his joy went and sold all he had and bought that field. Again, the kingdom of heaven is like a merchant looking for fine pearls. When he found one of great value, he went away and sold everything he had and bought it." (Matthew 13:44–46)

For us to regain the kind of impact we read about that Christianity had on culture at its inception, we must recover the message and challenge that they preached. Jesus told us we must *count the cost* of being His disciple. Counting the cost means that we consider the claims of Christ and yield our lives to Him in full obedience. This is the very opposite of the common presentation that calls us to pray a quick prayer or walk down an aisle and make a public confession of our belief in Christ. Going back to the words of Jesus, we find a critical aspect of the presentation of the gospel that we may have failed to mention.

"Suppose one of you wants to build a tower. Won't you first sit down and estimate the cost to see if you have enough money to complete it? For if you lay the foundation and are not able to finish it, everyone who sees it will ridicule you, saying, 'This person began to build and wasn't able to finish.'" (Luke 14:28–30)

Counting the cost means seriously and thoughtfully understanding the full implications of our commitment. It means we give up not only our wrongs but also our rights. Everyone today seems quite concerned about their societal rights; however, we are called to yield to God's way. We are now following Him; He is not following us.

Usually people hear messages about all the blessings of being a Christian, and, assuredly, there are many. It is also common to hear testimonies about how following Christ has given people real peace and joy. The subjective sense of the value of faith has definitely been heralded as the primary reason to believe.

Yet when you read the accounts of people coming to a place of faith in Christ in the New Testament, the message they heard was slightly different. They were told of hardship and suffering that would accompany their decision. Take for example the apostle Paul. The message he was initially told would be unheard-of in our Western context. "But the Lord said to Ananias, 'Go! This man is my chosen instrument to proclaim my name to the Gentiles and their kings and to the people of Israel. I will show him how much he must suffer for my name'" (Acts 9:15–16). In light of this reality we must understand not just the historical truth of the Christian faith but the proper response we must have if we truly believe. Here are a few critical dimensions of this response that might seem odd to most ears but will produce the kind of life you're really looking for.

1. Deny Yourself

Then he called the crowd to him along with his disciples and said: "Whoever wants to be my disciple must deny themselves and take up their cross and follow me. For whoever wants to save their life will lose it, but whoever loses their life for me and for the gospel will save it. What good is it for someone to gain the whole world, yet forfeit their soul? Or what can anyone give in exchange for their soul?"

—Mark 8:34–37

It seems counterintuitive, but if we want to find true life we must yield our lives first. We must first lose in order to win. This message is so absent from the vocabulary of the modern Christian presentation that it might sound harsh and unrealistic to some. However, it was the message Jesus gave out clearly and without apology. It presupposes that you know Jesus is Lord and that He died and rose again. Because this is true, obeying Him fully is the only response.

The essence of self-denial is to acknowledge that God's ways are higher than ours. To deny ourselves means that we are no longer leaning to our feelings, appetites, and fleshly proclivities. For instance, if someone offends you deeply, the normal reaction is to hold a grudge and seek revenge. The problem with this response is that Jesus commands us to forgive others and love them instead. If you deny yourself in this case, you are denying your "right" to remain angry and bitter, partly because it was never a right to begin with. Instead, you now choose God's way and forgive the person from your heart. It doesn't always make sense to our feelings, but it yields peace and reconciliation.

> "For my thoughts are not your thoughts,
>> neither are your ways my ways,"
>>> declares the LORD.
> "As the heavens are higher than the earth,
>> so are my ways higher than your ways
>> and my thoughts than your thoughts." (Isaiah 55:8–9)

This applies to any kind of temptation where what we feel like doing is in conflict with the expressed will of God. Take for instance the area of sexual purity. The Bible is clear that God's will is for us to be pure and holy, to abstain from sexual activity until marriage. Though this may be ignored by many today, it doesn't change the truth or alter our need to deny ourselves and obey Christ.

> It is God's will that you should be sanctified: that you should avoid sexual immorality; that each of you should learn to control your own body in a way that is holy and honorable, not in passionate lust like the pagans, who do not know God; and that in this matter no one should wrong or take advantage of a brother or sister. The Lord will punish all those who commit such sins, as we told you and warned you before. For God did not call us to be impure, but to live a holy life. Therefore, anyone who rejects this instruction does not reject a human being but God, the very God who gives you his Holy Spirit. (1 Thessalonians 4:3–8)

2. Pick Up Your Cross

> Then he called the crowd to him along with his disciples and said: "Whoever wants to be my disciple must deny themselves and take up their cross and follow me. For whoever wants to save their life will lose it, but whoever loses their life for me and for the gospel will save it."
>
> —Mark 8:34–35

For most in the West, the cost of following Christ is simply surrendering the things they know are wrong or sinful. This is a progressive process that begins with giving up the things that are glaringly wrong and gradually relinquishing the secret areas in the deepest part of our inner thoughts, attitudes, and motives. When

Christ calls us to follow Him, He tells us to pick up our own cross. That can seem a little strange to our ears, especially when crucifixion is no longer a part of our cultural experience. Carrying our cross means that we stay in a place of submission and obedience to God's will, not our own. We don't outgrow this place of humility and surrender to God. The apostle Paul is the prime example of someone who was dramatically transformed by this amazing grace of Jesus Christ. He explicitly testifies of how his life came to end in a spiritual sense for his new life to begin: "I have been crucified with Christ and I no longer live, but Christ lives in me. The life I now live in the body, I live by faith in the Son of God, who loved me and gave himself for me" (Galatians 2:20).

At the cross of Christ, our sins were paid for in full. Our response is to live our lives in the shadow of that example of surrender and submission that Christ modeled. He would sweat drops of blood as He faced the ultimate temptation to abandon God's plan because of the pain and suffering that lay ahead. Instead He prayed, "Yet not what I will, but what you will" (Mark 14:36).

3. Following Him

In World War II, Germany was led by a maniacal leader who expanded its borders through aggression and terror. Much of the German church capitulated under the enormous weight of intimidation and force that would control millions and murder millions more. Despite the fact that many cowered under the specter of the Nazis' tactics, there was a remnant of believers in Germany who refused to compromise, regardless of the cost to them personally. Dietrich Bonhoeffer was one such leader who resisted the evil regime and eventually paid for this stand with his own life. In his classic book *The Cost of Discipleship*, Bonhoeffer said the call of Christ demands that we surrender all to obtain the life of Christ. He eschewed the folly and emptiness of cheap grace and boldly proclaimed what many today would call an oxymoron: costly grace.

> It is costly because it costs a man his life, and it is grace because it gives a man the only true life. It is costly because it condemns sin, and it is grace because it justifies the sinner. Above all, it is *costly* because it cost God the life of his Son: "you were bought at a price" (1 Corinthians 6:20), and what has cost God much cannot be cheap for us. Above all, it is *grace* because God did not reckon his Son too dear a price to pay for our lives but delivered him up for us.[5]

Jesus simply said, "Follow Me." These words still reverberate today. To follow Him is to follow His word and His ways. We follow Him into the greatest adventure imaginable of reaching the world with the gospel.

THE CONFLICT FACING THE BELIEVER

There is not only a cost of following Christ but also a *conflict* into which we are called. There is a spiritual battle raging over the hearts and minds of nations: "For our struggle is not against flesh and blood, but against the rulers, against the authorities, against the powers of this dark world and against the spiritual forces of evil in the heavenly realms" (Ephesians 6:12). To fail to mention this is to not be faithful or truthful in our gospel message. What is the source of this conflict? Here are four of the most obvious reasons:

1. Darkness Hates the Light

We are told that there is no fellowship between light and darkness and that people hate the light because their deeds are evil and the light exposes them. The apostle John wrote not only a gospel but also several smaller letters. He said,

> This is the message we have heard from him and declare to you: God is light; in him there is no darkness at all. If we claim to have fellowship with him, and yet walk in the darkness, we lie and do not live out the truth. But if we walk in the light, as he is in the light, we have fellowship with one another, and the blood of Jesus, his Son, purifies us from all sin. (1 John 1:5–7)

If you're in the dark and someone turns on an intense light, it can be extremely painful. Christ is the light that enlightens every person (John 1:9). As He fills our hearts, the darkness must leave.

2. The Exclusive Claims of Christ

Jesus answered, "I am the way and the truth and the life. No one comes to the Father except through me."

—John 14:6

Christ is the exclusive representative of God. His resurrection from the dead separated Him from all others that would claim to be God's mouthpiece. This seems narrow-minded and intolerant to many. There is ultimately no blending of all religions into one giant soup of spirituality.

This doesn't mean there aren't good things in other religions. All truth is from God and can be expressed by anyone, including atheists. The difference is that Christ is the highest authority in the universe. His name is exalted above every other name. "Salvation is found in no one else, for there is no other name under heaven given to mankind by which we must be saved" (Acts 4:12).

3. The Struggle Is Against Immorality, Not Just Unbelief

> Dear friends, I urge you, as foreigners and exiles, to abstain from sinful desires, which wage war against your soul.
>
> —1 Peter 2:11

Many skeptics try and hide behind the façade that their objections are purely intellectual when, in actuality, it is a deeper moral struggle that's at work. The bottom line is that they refuse to recognize any authority above their own when it comes to their moral and, specifically, their sexual practices and preferences. The Bible is filled with warnings against immoral behavior and the consequences that follow. There is an internal battle inside of us all. The Scriptures tell us that this battle is between the sinful human nature (our fleshly desires) and the Spirit and His desires. But we are destined to win this battle because of the power of the Spirit within us as believers:

> Those who live according to the flesh have their minds set on what the flesh desires; but those who live in accordance with the Spirit have their minds set on what the Spirit desires. The mind governed by the flesh is death, but the mind governed by the Spirit is life and peace. The mind governed by the flesh is hostile to God; it does not submit to God's law, nor can it do so. Those who are in the realm of the flesh cannot please God.
>
> You, however, are not in the realm of the flesh but are in

the realm of the Spirit, if indeed the Spirit of God lives in you. (Romans 8:5–9)

4. The Existence of a Spiritual Enemy of God and His Purposes

The god of this age has blinded the minds of unbelievers, so that they cannot see the light of the gospel that displays the glory of Christ, who is the image of God.

—2 Corinthians 4:4

From the very beginning of humanity, there has been an ancient foe that has tempted, deceived, and destroyed those who fall under his power. This indeed is Satan. Far from the impish character in a red suit and pitchfork, he is called in other places an angel of light. In other words, he comes to seduce and lure us into captivity and often dresses himself to do so.

Jesus' ministry began with casting out demons and healing those who were in bondage to this malevolent power. It is vital to know that Satan is not omnipresent but is likewise a finite created being. Jesus has given us authority over his works and has triumphed over him in life and in His death on the cross. "God anointed Jesus of Nazareth with the Holy Spirit and power, and . . . he went around doing good and healing all who were under the power of the devil, because God was with him" (Acts 10:38).

A CHILLING PREDICTION

When people cite hypocrisy among believers as their reason for rejecting the truth of Christianity, they fail to realize that Jesus actually foretold that there would be imposters and hypocrites who would claim His name.

> "Watch out for false prophets. They come to you in sheep's clothing, but inwardly they are ferocious wolves. By their fruit you will recognize them. Do people pick grapes from thornbushes, or figs from thistles? Likewise, every good tree bears good fruit, but a bad tree bears bad fruit. A good tree cannot bear bad fruit, and a bad tree cannot bear good fruit. Every tree that does not bear good fruit is cut down and thrown into the fire. Thus, by their fruit you will recognize them."
> (Matthew 7:15–20)

While there is no way to guarantee that people will always follow God faithfully, steps can be taken to minimize the risk of their failing and falling away. This brings us to the place where all of this knowledge about the reality of the existence of God and His Son Jesus Christ calls us into what has been referred to as the Great Commission. This is the last command Christ gave to His disciples to spread His gospel to the entire planet.

THE COMMAND TO MAKE DISCIPLES

> "Therefore go and make disciples of all nations, baptizing them in the name of the Father and of the Son and of the Holy Spirit."
> —Matthew 28:19

Steve Murrell was one of my college roommates and moved to Manila in 1984 to establish a church that emphasized reaching university students. Today that congregation has grown to more than eighty thousand members, meeting in fifteen locations throughout the city. Steve and his team have authored and modeled the four *E*s (engage, establish, equip, and empower). Steve explains:

> We have identified four principles that serve as the foundation of what we believe and practice about discipleship. These principles are not unique to our context, but, like all principles, they are true for all time and in all places. Some people use different words and phrases, but the principles are the same. All four are essential. If one is removed, the discipleship process breaks down. We call these four principles the Four *E*s—engage, establish, equip, and empower.[6]

Engage Unbelievers

This means we learn to effectively and faithfully approach people with the gospel and the powerful truths of the Christian faith. This is such an important area of ministry that we devote the last chapter (10) to the subject. What we discuss briefly here is the priority Jesus placed on reaching out to people who were yet to believe. The Scripture refers to them as unbelievers, doubters, and the lost. Modern sensitivities have caused many to adopt softer language that is less offensive in describing those who are yet to believe: pre-Christian, unreached, seekers, and so forth. Regardless of the words you use, the reality remains that there are people who do not know the Lord and will suffer judgment of eternal separation from God as a result. The mandate to "go into all the world and make disciples of all nations" is still in effect.

The most important work we can be involved in is the labor of serving others and helping to bring them the truth of the knowledge of God, Christ, and salvation. As Jesus said, "For the Son of Man came to seek and to save the lost" (Luke 19:10).

Regardless of how successful or prosperous people may appear, there is spiritual poverty blanketing billions in the world. In spite of living in the most innovative and technologically spectacular time in history, we seem to be unable to acknowledge our deep need for God and His ways.

The Engaging Church

We mentioned in the beginning of this book that there is a crisis in Christianity, especially in the West. The church is losing people who self-identify as Christians and there is a rising trend of others saying they have no religious affiliation. There is a growing awareness that there is no clear process for teaching people how to communicate their faith to others. As we saw in earlier chapters, the church experienced dynamic growth in the first three hundred years. The clear, simple message of the good news that Jesus was the Messiah and had been raised from the dead to verify that identity compelled believers to tell others regardless of the persecution or resistance they would encounter.

The call to preach the gospel is the command to proclaim God's truth to every person in every nation. It is a daunting task to consider. Because this directive was given by Jesus, it should be the primary task of every believer, not just pastors, evangelists, or religious professionals. In fact, studies have shown that the majority of people who become Christians do so because of the influence of a relative or a friend. Ultimately, they were able to help others because they had been helped themselves by their connection to a local church. The church is the place where the training and equipping takes place.

Jesus promised to build His church and the gates of hell would not prevail. As much as reports say people are leaving the church—God isn't. The church is still His primary plan and purpose in the earth. Jesus said, "I will build My church, and the gates of Hades shall not prevail against it" (Matthew 16:18 NKJV).

There are so many wonderful projects and programs that are a part of the typical congregation. In spite of all the great works of service, the centerpiece of the original mission and charge of Jesus to make disciples of all nations is often left out. That's why we have tried to bring awareness and focus to helping the church regain this cutting edge. Everyone wants to feel they are a part of a great church. Understand and remember what a great church should look like: it must have great evangelism—a process that is intentional, repeatable, and transferable.

In the next chapter we discuss intentional evangelism and the apologetic training process in detail.

Establish Foundations

"Why do you call me, 'Lord, Lord,' and do not do what I say? As for everyone who comes to me and hears my words and puts them into practice, I will show you what they are like. They are like a man building a house, who dug down deep and laid the foundation on rock. When a flood came, the torrent struck that house but could not shake it, because it was well built."

—Luke 6:46–48

Anyone who has seen a building going up knows the importance of digging deep to properly lay a strong foundation. When foundations are weak or poorly constructed, the storms of life can easily topple the building. This is seen in the way people assume that praying a prayer and asking Jesus into their hearts is all that is needed. When the apostles preached the gospel, the people asked what they should do in response. They would tell them to repent (turn) and believe. Steve Murrell agrees with this concept: "Strong foundations that withstand the storms are constructed not only with the doctrine of the Word but also with the disciplines of following Christ and His Word. For example, it is not enough to merely teach about the preeminence of Christ; we must also challenge young believers to practice repentance and live a life of daily submission to His Lordship in all areas of life."[7]

A solid foundation consists of repentance as well as faith. Charles Spurgeon once said that conversion is like a two-sided coin. On one side is repentance and the other faith.[8] If you truly turn to Christ in faith, you necessarily turn from everything else you are trusting in. In fact, the apostle Paul testified that Christ appeared to him on the road to Damascus and instructed him to declare this kind of message, "I am sending you to them to open their eyes and turn them from darkness to light, and from the power of Satan to God, so that they may receive forgiveness of sins and a place among those who are sanctified by faith in me" (Acts 26:17–18).

Together, Steve Murrell and I coauthored *The Purple Book*, a study guide that helps ensure these foundations are solid. With more than one million in print, in twenty-six languages, this guide is like a tool that helps you dig down deep and lay the foundations of the faith on the solid rock of Christ. In the preface this charge is given, "We must dig down deep and tear out everything that is hostile to Christ. We must hear his words—particularly those that deal with the very foundations of faith—and obey."[9]

Equip Believers

And he gave the apostles, the prophets, the evangelists, the
shepherds and teachers, to equip the saints for the work of
ministry, for building up the body of Christ.

—Ephesians 4:11–12 ESV

This tells us that the primary purpose of those who are full-
time or professional ministers is to equip people for the work of
ministry, not to do all the ministry themselves. This is why making disciples involves training and equipping people to minister.
This shifts the focus dramatically on the part of those who serve
as leaders.

We hear the phrase all the time: "Every member a minister." Yet because of our performance-driven culture, we often
have little tolerance for the messiness of the equipping process. We do church as if only professional ministers should
do ministry. The biblical job description for professional
ministers—apostles, prophets, evangelists, pastors, and teachers—is to equip the "non-pros" for ministry, then get out of
their way. When we forget that, we forget one of the primary
reasons God called us to serve in the first place.[10]

We equip people by helping them understand their own gifts,
calling, and purpose. Helping someone discover his or her God-
given purpose is vital to growth and emotional well-being. If you
have a keen sense of your purpose in life, you will usually make
it through the struggles and hard times that await us all. It's no
surprise that the book *The Purpose Driven Life* became one of the
bestselling books of all time.

It is also important to help them learn to understand the Word of God. It is God's Word that helps them overcome sin and temptation as well as guide them in the path of wisdom. The essence of the equipping process is to help people become skilled at using the Scriptures like a sharp sword being used in a conflict. "All Scripture is God-breathed and is useful for teaching, rebuking, correcting and training in righteousness, so that the servant of God may be thoroughly equipped for every good work" (2 Timothy 3:16–17).

One of the many faithful pastors in America is Dale Evrist in Nashville, Tennessee. He leads his congregation through the Bible every year from cover to cover. He has a daily fifteen-minute podcast called *Walking Through the Word* that helps believers get grounded in the key truths of the Scripture. He told me in an interview, "There is no doubt that much of the confusion in hearts and minds of people who call themselves Christians could be cleared up by simply consistently reading the Bible. It is incredible the amount of deception that comes in when people are left to their own feelings and instincts rather than trusting in the very truth that brought the universe into existence."[11]

We also equip them by helping them learn to minister to others. It is physically impossible for the millions of people who need spiritual help and encouragement to get this from just listening to sermons and podcasts and reading books. They eventually will need a real person to sit with them and help them. Much of the time, it's simply our friendship and willingness to listen that can make a huge difference. Obviously, there are serious issues people face that need the attention of senior leaders and elders, but for the most part there are general areas of encouragement and instruction that all believers should be capable of sharing with others.

Empower Disciples

"Very truly I tell you, whoever believes in me will do the works
I have been doing, and they will do even greater things than
these, because I am going to the Father."

—John 14:12

The last step in this simple process of discipleship is that of
empowering people to do what they've been called to do. Jesus
had twelve disciples who initially followed Him and watched
Him perform mighty works and literally change the world wherever He went. Then the time came that He empowered them and
commissioned them to go and do greater works than they had
seen Him do. As Steve Murrell states,

> Jesus was never content for disciples to simply follow Him as
> spectators but was intent on empowering them to do what He
> had been doing. He went so far as to say that they would do
> even greater works after He had gone back to the Father. It was
> one thing to follow Jesus, but standing in for Him as a minis-
> ter was something else altogether. What thoughts must have
> run through the minds of the twelve when Jesus said, "OK,
> now I am sending you out to do what I have been doing."[12]

Imagine getting a job working for the wealthiest, wisest man
and woman alive. They interview you and tell you that they see
great potential in you and they want to help develop it and make
you successful. You tell them what you have thought you should
do with your life, but they offer you a compelling vision of what
best matches your talents and abilities. In fact, they help you see
areas in your life that you had no idea you would excel in. On

top of this they promise to mentor you personally to see all of the things they've described become a reality. Most would consider this an incredible privilege and honor. To not consider this kind of opportunity would seem foolish to most people.

Now imagine this: the Creator of the universe, the all-wise and all-knowing God, wants to build a relationship with you. He obviously has the greatest insight into your strengths and weaknesses and offers to help you maximize your gifts and talents to help change the world. Would you see this as oppressive and controlling or as something far more incredible than being helped by the smartest or wealthiest person alive?

This is the mind-set we need to instill in others. God uses people to help in the process of His pouring His wisdom and love into His creation. I am so grateful for the many people who have made a difference in my life by pouring into me and then releasing me to go and make a difference.

As one of the most empowering leaders I know, Joey Bonafacio from Manila, wrote, "Everyone—man, woman, young, old, rich, poor—should be a disciple who makes disciples. This is the hope of the nations and the way to transform the world one person at a time. To this mission Jesus promised we would be empowered, saying, 'Surely I am with you always, to the very end of the age.'"[13]

SUMMARY

Capturing what it means to be a follower of Christ is extremely challenging—especially in one brief overview. While the pictures of those who are facing threats against their lives is one clear image of the challenges you may face, there is also the image of incredible joy and peace. This is what I was drawn to, a people filled with a love for God and one another. There is also the promise of power to help others. Jesus said, "You will receive power when the Holy Spirit has come on you" (Acts 1:8 NKJV).

We have examined a simple four-step process that can be a guide in fulfilling the Lord's command to make disciples of all nations. It is represented by four words that in English start with the letter E: *engage, establish, equip,* and *empower.*

We are called to engage unbelievers with the gospel, establish biblical foundations in their lives and help them learn God's Word, equip them to do the work of the ministry, and empower them to fulfill their God-given purpose.

Steve Murrell, whose three sons played tennis in college, has logged many hours in the stands watching them practice and play endless matches. He recounts the wisdom of one of their son's coaches, who constantly encouraged his players to never get tired of the same old boring tennis strokes they were making:

> Coach Tom would say, "You wanna win? Then you have to master the same ole boring strokes. Up, down, up. That's how you create topspin, and topspin is your friend. Nothing fancy. Same ole boring strokes!" I think I lead the church the same way Tom coaches tennis. You want to make disciples? It doesn't require anything fancy. Just the same ole boring strokes: engage, establish, equip, empower. Engage, establish, equip, empower. Engage, establish, equip, empower. And that's about all we have been doing at Victory since 1984. The same ole boring strokes.[14]

10

DEFENDERS OF
THE FAITH

Prepared to Share the Gospel

*If the children view themselves as Christians, it is probably
not because they have studied the facts and come to a
point of intellectual conviction but because their family is
Christian, so they believe they must be Christians also.*[1]
—BOB BELTZ

THE DYSTOPIAN VISION OF THE WORLD TO COME,
found in novels such as *Hunger Games, Divergent,* and *Maze
Runner,* predicts a coming day when totalitarian governments
will have virtually eliminated all individual freedoms to ensure a
very rigid and artificial peace. Dominated by the Orwellian idea
of an all-seeing and controlling power usurping the freedoms of
the individual, any attitude or impulse to the contrary is ruthlessly
and quickly eliminated. Yet in every case, a hero emerges to battle
the overwhelming odds and deliver people from the bondage and
control of an ultimately malevolent and suffocating enemy. It is

usually young people who come to a knowledge of what is really true and learn to battle the forces of darkness against overwhelming odds and win. J. R. R. Tolkien and C. S. Lewis created stories like *Lord of the Rings* and The Chronicles of Narnia that told of grave challenges and incredible odds as well. Reluctant and unlikely young people were called on to rise up and act heroically and courageously to push back the encroaching darkness.

These stories are inspiring and challenging, but they are just that, stories. For followers of Christ, this struggle is no fairy tale. The real-life version of this scenario is seen in the Christian call to proclaim the truth of the gospel and, in doing so, set captives free from the spiritual bondage and control of forces more insidious and deceptive than any depicted in the movies. In this cosmic struggle of good versus evil, there is no neutral corner. All must decide where they stand, what they believe, and how they can make a difference in their generation.

This call to change the world captivated my imagination during my senior year in college. There was no other job or opportunity that pressed on my heart more urgently than the need for people to know Christ. It was the transformation of my skeptical older brother during his third year of law school that had dramatically demonstrated to me the difference the truth of Christ can make on those that seem farthest away from God. I remember saying, "If God can change him, He can change anybody."

For more than thirty years I have focused on reaching university students. Today our ministry is reaching hundreds of university campuses in more than sixty nations. We have been inspired by so many that have gone before us and shown how open young people are to a credible presentation of the gospel and the truth of the Christian faith. Statistics of how many young people are walking away from their faith once they leave home for college makes the urgent case for training as many as possible, as quickly as possible.

Every Believer Needs to Be Engaged in This Learning Process

I've had the privilege of being mentored and taught by some of the best Christian minds on the planet. It is humbling to me to be in the presence of men and women who have dedicated their hearts and minds to communicating the truth of the faith using their academic platform or profession. For some reason, much of their great wisdom and writing doesn't often make it down to the grass-roots level and make the impact that it could on the average believer. The hope is that this material will make this important knowledge accessible to believers of all walks of life.

As we mentioned in the previous chapter, the first aspect of discipleship is engaging people with the truth of the gospel. In this chapter we hope to bring all that we have discussed in this book (as well as in *God's Not Dead*) into practical focus so that the information and revelation of its truths can be clearly communicated to others.

Evangelism and Apologetics Are Connected

When I first heard the word *apologetics*, it sounded like Christians should apologize for their bad behavior and hypocrisy. That's all

I had known growing up when attending church. When I think of some of the terrible things I learned while being involved in church functions and events, it still makes me mad. There was actually a collection of pornographic magazines under the staircase of the youth hall in the church I attended in my elementary school days. There was virtually no difference in the lives of people who attended church and those who didn't. This kind of experience turned my older brother into an atheist and simply confirmed to me that the immoral lifestyle I would adopt a few years later was okay and acceptable.

But apologetics isn't about apologizing for the failings of people who claim to be Christians. It's about giving the reasons for your faith. In other words, you are making a defense. The Greek word *apologia* occurs in 1 Peter 3:15, where it states, "Always be prepared to give an answer to everyone who asks you to give the reason for the hope that you have. But do this with gentleness and respect." As we will soon discuss, the last part of that verse is just as important as the first.

I remember the impact reading *Evidence that Demands a Verdict* by Josh McDowell had on me years ago. The fact that there was real evidence for the reliability of the Bible and the resurrection of Jesus gave me enough confidence to engage university students and try to help them unravel the entanglements of unbelief in which they were trapped. I may not have known a lot, but the little I did know at least kept me from being swept away by the flash floods of skepticism that are so common on a college campus.

I then discovered verses like 2 Corinthians 10:3–5: "For though we live in the world, we do not wage war as the world does. The weapons we fight with are not the weapons of the world. On the contrary, they have divine power to demolish strongholds. We demolish arguments and every pretension that sets itself up against the knowledge of God, and we take captive every thought to make it obedient to Christ." The strongholds spoken of here are referring to the intellectual strongholds in people's minds. We are called to demolish those strongholds with the knowledge of Christ. It then says that we are to "take every thought captive" to the obedience of that knowledge. The reason we are to take every thought captive is because it only takes one erroneous thought to take you captive.

Time and time again in conversations with believers and unbelievers alike, the testimony is consistent that they either came to Christ or fell away into unbelief because of a few thoughts that seemed to change their worldview almost over-night. Ignorance of God's truth results in your being susceptible to almost any and every kind of deception. Conversely, the knowledge of God can serve as a positive stronghold, yielding peace and courage. The winds of change sweep Western culture, causing massive confusion in the areas of sexual ethics and even gender identity. This is a testimony to the tragic lack of truth needed to adequately anchor our personal lives as well as our societies.

THE FULL ARMOR OF GOD

Finally, be strong in the Lord and in his mighty power. Put on the full armor of God, so that you can take your stand against the devil's schemes.

—Ephesians 6:10–11

Before going out to help others, you must be prepared for the conflict. This admonition about wearing the armor of God is not just a nice Sunday school lesson. Many have tried to minister to others and have not been prepared to handle the objections to the faith that are raised. On top of that is the fact that this is not just an intellectual struggle, as the opening text mentions; it is very much a spiritual conflict. It takes preparation to be able to withstand the onslaught that has caused others to defect and leave the faith. It's like going into an area contaminated by a deadly virus. You see workers from the CDC wearing protective suits to keep them from being affected by the viruses and contaminants that have devastated others. In a way, the armor of God is like that protective suit. The defensive components listed in the verses following the passage above talk about the helmet of salvation, the sword of the Spirit, and the shield of faith to extinguish all the fiery darts of the evil one (vv. 14–18).

During the writing of this book, as well as *God's Not Dead*, I spent hundreds of hours listening to skeptical presentations and reading books from the most committed atheist thinkers of our day. As I pored over their writings, I made sure that no doubts or accusations against God's truth remained unchallenged in my own heart and mind. It was a difficult task to listen to countless comments given for the express purpose of deliberately and viciously discrediting the Christian faith and then thoroughly research and respond to the underlying arguments. At times I had to use the shield of faith to extinguish the doubtful aftertaste that accompanied these writings. I reminded myself that no one is truly objective. I am not and the skeptics sure are not. I have done my best to be forthright and say that my motive in writing this book is to help people believe that Jesus Christ is the Son of

God. Just as the apostle John said, "These are written that you may believe that Jesus is the Christ, the Son of God, and that believing you may have life in His name" (John 20:31 NKJV).

In chapter 9, we looked at being a disciple of Jesus, first and foremost. All of the aspects of being connected to a group of fellow believers, being equipped, trained, and learning to walk out the teachings of Christ in an open and transparent environment, must be a part of your life before you can consistently launch out and help others. Jesus sent out His disciples in pairs. There is no shame in realizing that we need others in our lives to help us. With this kind of solid foundation, we can confidently help others.

When I became a Christian in college, I was privileged to have a small group of Christian friends and a campus church that I could be a part of. That little group of people was a lifeline to me in those early days. Being able to have others that I could share my struggles with and also learn from kept me growing spiritually instead of falling away. There were many days when the strength and accountability of my roommates kept me from becoming a casualty due to the constant opposition I faced at my school. Not only was I able to survive, I was able to begin helping others. It was because of this kind of support that I was able to help many members of my family come to faith in Christ as well as other lifelong friends of mine.

After graduation I embarked on a ministry of establishing Christian congregations in campus communities around the world. The essence of these communities was patterned after what I had benefited from and experienced during my college days. These types of things are usually missing when reading books on apologetics. People want to start with presenting the evidence for God and the shortcomings of the skeptics' challenges. But first, we must be solid followers of Christ to be His best witnesses to others. Because the goal of our efforts is to bring unbelievers to faith in Christ, they have to join a community of believers in order to grow and be protected and nurtured as their faith develops. If we never commit to a fellowship of believers, we are not likely to influence those we are trying to help.

In addition, congregations must learn to be places where evangelism and apologetics are a part of their very fabric. It is impossible to grow spiritually without learning to help others come to the place of faith. It's a strange phenomenon, but the more you help others, the stronger your faith becomes. Knowing this truth has led me to devote a significant segment of my time to helping people, as well as churches, learn to share and defend the truth of the Christian faith.

THE MISSING GIFT—EVANGELISTS

I came to the realization early in my Christian life that I was called as an evangelist. This gift is mentioned in Scripture as one of the primary gifts God has given the church to help people grow spiritually. "So Christ himself gave the apostles, the prophets, the evangelists, the pastors and teachers, to equip his people for works of service, so that the body of Christ may be built up until we all reach unity in the faith and in the knowledge of the Son of God and become mature, attaining to the whole measure of the fullness of Christ" (Ephesians 4:11–13). Evangelists are the women and men who are gifted by God to help model effective evangelism and equip believers to become fruitful communicators of the gospel. In order to have a missional church, you must have this gift that God has specifically given to make that desire a reality. Evangelists act like coaches in helping you to sustain the momentum gained through putting these principles into practice.

My doctoral dissertation at Fuller Theological Seminary was "The Gift of the Evangelist." When it was published in 2010, I was told it was the first doctoral dissertation in the world on that gift. I was stunned at that realization. There were hundreds of dissertations and studies on evangelism itself, of course, but none (that we knew of) on the specific gift that God had given to make evangelism a reality. The gift of the evangelist was given to the church to equip God's people to evangelize. If that gift is not in operation, the result will be a lack of fruitfulness in that area. This is exactly what the statistics are telling us.

I take the moment to mention evangelists because those who are apologists usually have this gift and calling. They are passionate about training as many as possible to understand the core beliefs of the faith and the reasons they are true. Apologists also tend to be teachers as well, but the overwhelming number of them yearn to see people come to the knowledge of the truth and be saved.

One of the largest churches in the world is in Manila, Philippines. They have more than eighty thousand people in attendance with more than eight thousand small groups that meet during the week. The senior minister of the congregation is Ferdie Cabiling. He came to Christ in the summer of 1984 when the congregation was established during a summer outreach program consisting of fifty-nine American students and one Canadian who came for a one-month missions trip. The congregation has grown exponentially from that time for many reasons. In Ferdie's opinion, the growth has been astounding because all the congregations and leaders in the city have remained focused on evangelism and outreach. He states, "Our congregation was birthed because evangelists came and preached the Gospel to us. That same passion still is present in our midst. As an evangelist and leader, it is my number one goal to make sure we stay true to Christ's final charge to preach the Gospel and make disciples of all nations."[2]

In the United States, there is also notable growth when the gift of the evangelist is identified and mobilizted to function alongside pastors and teachers in the local church. From smaller churches to larger ones, there is a notable difference when the evangelists are recognized and released to become a part of the ministry team. We call this "an engaging church" because the people in it have been prepared and equipped to help others.

The Process of Engagement

This brings us to the place of spelling out as clearly as possible the necessary ingredients for a successful evangelism and apologetics culture to emerge—both in churches and in the lives of ordinary believers. Most of the important things we learn are systemized so they can be repeated again and again and ultimately become second nature. You see this in terms of our early education where the basics of the alphabet and math are presented to us in memorable, repeatable lessons. I actually learned the Hebrew alphabet by hearing a song on a Barney (the purple dinosaur) children's video. Once something can be put in a clear process, it also becomes easier to teach others. This is critical to grasp when it comes to evangelism and apologetics. There are massive amounts of information available on these crucial topics, yet with all the knowledge available, the majority of Christians are virtually clueless when it comes to explaining why the Christian faith is true. Most default to the position of defending their "right to believe" rather than being able to show that what they believe is right.

I have spent years trying to make evangelism and apologetics both simple and clear. Much of the time the messages on evangelism are focused on the mandate from Scripture to preach the gospel to all nations. This indeed must be taught. But most never present a clear path to accomplish this goal. The lack of clarity in terms of any type of training process leaves the majority of Christians in a place of ineffectiveness and frustration when it comes to evangelism, and even more angst when it comes to being able to present any evidence for the truth of their faith.

Christians, for the most part, are at a loss about how to have a credible course correction and reverse the negative trends when they are advancing the cause of Christ. It points to a massive gap that exists in most places when it comes to any kind of intentional evangelism and apologetic process.

If you've ever played golf, you know that a few minor changes can make a major difference in your scoring, which reduces your frustration levels and keeps you from giving up the game. Most have given up on evangelism because they feel the similar frustration and futility and just assume that this kind of thing should be done by religious professionals. If this mentality is not changed, then we are fighting a lost cause. It will be impossible to reach the world for Christ with only full-time ministers involved in the process.

The principles we are about to discuss may seem simple, but they have produced results when faithfully put into practice. I've tried to clarify this process and reduce it to five essential steps. They are the key ingredients of the recipe that can make any individual a faithful witness and any congregation a place of dynamic outreach to non-Christians.

To help you remember these vital ingredients to having an intentional evangelism process, here are two key words: *great* and *salt*. The word *great* applies to the overall process that we are recommending and the word *salt* to a key dimension that has changed evangelism from an awkward burden to an enjoyable and even an extraordinary experience.

I was inspired to use the word *great* as a memory device for this evangelism process by a verse that described the ministry of John the Baptist. When the angel Gabriel foretold of his birth and his role as the forerunner for the Messiah, he said, "He will be great in the sight of the Lord. . . . He will turn many of the children of Israel to the Lord their God" (Luke 1:15–16 NKJV). John's greatness would be in his character and his ability to turn people back to God. This is reminiscent of the words from what many scholars think was the same angel who came to the prophet Daniel more than five hundred years earlier and said, "Multitudes who sleep in the dust of the earth will awake: some to everlasting life, others to shame and everlasting contempt. Those who are wise will shine like the brightness of the heavens, and those who lead many to righteousness, like the stars for ever and ever" (Daniel 12:2–3).

Make no mistake. God cares about people coming to know Him and promises to bless those who are willing to be instruments

He can use in that process. There are certainly many other ways to please God, but I believe none is more important than the communication of the gospel to others. As Jesus said, "For the Son of Man came to seek and to save the lost" (Luke 19:10).

GOSPEL

Everything starts with a clear grasp of the gospel. There have been volumes written on all aspects of what it means and its range of impact. Here, we are talking about *memorizing* and *mastering* a clear definition of what the gospel is. If you are able to clearly articulate the gospel in a conversation, you will be able to offer a person a reasonable chance at understanding and accepting its message.

Often when you ask a Christian to tell you what the gospel is, you get a wide variety of answers. If these were directions to a destination, you would probably get lost. We have found that when you teach people to clearly articulate the gospel, it dramatically boosts their confidence and the probability that they will tell it to someone else. Let's look again at our definition of gospel from chapter 4:

> The *gospel* is the good news that God became man in Jesus Christ. He lived the life we should have lived and died the death we should have died—in our place. Three days later He rose from the dead, proving that He is the Son of God and offering the gift of salvation to those who repent and believe in Him.

If you understand the meaning of this definition, which is a summary of different verses that are related to the essence of Christ's saving work accomplished on our behalf, then you will be able to help others while indeed helping yourself. By this I mean that in the gospel is the power to keep you safe, regardless of the spiritual opposition, as well as sustain you through the intellectual arguments against the Christian faith.

God became man in Jesus Christ. God stepped into the world by taking on human flesh. The religions of the world call men to ascend and work their way to God. Christianity explains that God came down to us.

He lived the life we should have lived. God expects us to keep the moral law. Christ lived a perfect life. His life modeled a life completely yielded to God. This was the life that God intended all men and women to live.

He died the death we should have died—in our place. This is a difficult truth for skeptics to embrace, that evil must be punished. If there is no consequence for breaking a law, then the law ceases to be a law. Christ bore our punishment by taking our place through His death on a Roman cross.

Three days later, He rose from the dead. Christ's resurrection from the dead verified His identity and proved that His authority was real. It also gives us hope that there is life after death. This further demonstrates His exclusive claim to be the true path to God.

He offers salvation and forgiveness of sins to those who repent and believe in Him. In God's gift of salvation we not only receive forgiveness of sins but also are delivered from the power of evil and its consequences—both in this life and the next. To repent means to turn from evil and from trusting in our own efforts to earn our own salvation. In turning from evil, we turn to Christ and believe. The promise is straightforward: "For God so loved the world that He gave His only begotten Son, that whoever believes in Him should not perish but have everlasting life" (John 3: 16 NKJV).

REASONS

More specifically, the *r* could be listed as *reasons to believe*. This is what apologetics is all about. We have already mentioned the key verse in 1 Peter 3:15, which calls us to give reasons for the hope we have. If you feel you have no need for apologetics, then chances are that you aren't engaging real unbelievers. It seems we are good at talking to Christians about being better Christians but not good at all in explaining the reasons for the validity of the faith to unbelievers.

This book has been about giving the reasons to believe that Jesus is indeed the Son of God and was resurrected in history to verify that claim. We've also given reasons to believe the gospel records are reliable and trustworthy. In the first book, *God's Not Dead*, the foundational evidences for God's existence were detailed. One of the most important statements we could make was "real faith isn't blind." We don't come to God against reason but through it. There isn't a lack of evidence keeping people from believing in God but an abundance of it that leaves us without excuse. This includes the beginning of the universe, the origin of life and morality, and the witness of God in history through Jesus Christ.

There are so many incredible resources in the area of apologetics that it's hard to know where to begin. C. S. Lewis's classic work *Mere Christianity* remains relevant after sixty years as a bestseller. Tim Keller's *The Reason for God* is another classic work written by one of America's most respected pastors and teachers. Many incredible scholars, such as Dr. Gary Habermas (who wrote the foreword to this book); Dr. Hugh Ross, an astrophysicist; and Dr. John Lennox, an Oxford mathematician and philosopher, have written outstanding books that speak to the most formidable intellectual challengers. Their writings speak as well to the young person struggling with doubts and fears.

Other notable people who are helping to equip the church are Stephen C. Meyer, PhD, from Cambridge, who is one of the main proponents of the Intelligent Design Movement; Dr. William Lane Craig, a philosopher and theologian, whose debates are viewed by millions on YouTube; Dr. Brian Miller, a PhD in physics, who was a vital part of this project; Dr. Frank Turek, an excellent debater in his own right; and J. Warner Wallace, a cold case detective, who came to faith from atheism after concluding the Gospels were indeed reliable eyewitness accounts. Also included in this list is Mary Jo Sharp, who is inspiring women to become leading voices in this crucial area of ministry. All of these, and countless more, have dedicated themselves to help empower people of all ages and educational backgrounds to become defenders of the faith.

There is also the need to help people understand the reasons why the Christian faith is true compared to the other religions and philosophies that compete for the hearts and minds of billions in the world today. I hope this book has helped you grasp why Jesus Christ is indeed God's ultimate revelation to humanity and the true guide to salvation and peace.

EMPATHY

Being empathetic should be a given in terms of evangelism. Empathy is about compassion, mercy, and, ultimately, the love of God toward others. At the heart of this process is having a heart for people. In a world where so much rancor and anger are displayed about the issues people are passionate about, having this kind of empathy is not an easy endeavor. In fact, it truly takes a supernatural work of grace in our hearts. It is so important that Dr. Sean McDowell of Biola University told me in an interview that his primary goal is to bring civility and dignity to those engaged in apologetics. "If you have the truth, then there is no need for anger or impatience with others. We must give our reasons to believe with the kindness and respect that people made in the image of God deserve."[3]

As the apostle Paul told Timothy,

And the Lord's servant must not be quarrelsome but must be kind to everyone, able to teach, not resentful. Opponents must be gently instructed, in the hope that God will grant them repentance leading them to a knowledge of the truth, and that they will come to their senses and escape from the trap of the devil, who has taken them captive to do his will. (2 Timothy 2:24–26)

Sure, there are nice people who don't care about God or evangelism. Their sunny dispositions come effortlessly. But they are the exception, not the rule. When you begin to reach out to people with the gospel and the evidence for the truth of the Christian faith, you are minimally inviting a potential argument or even a battle in some cases.

For me, it's the memory of the enormous struggle I came through before I became a follower of Christ that gives me the most empathy for those in need. When I talk to people who seem so far away from God, and many times not interested in knowing about these things, I get flashbacks of the way I used to be. It doesn't take much to stir my sense of empathy for their antagonistic disposition.

The more I read the Scripture, the more I see Jesus Himself reaching out with compassion to the unlikeliest of characters. It was scandalous to the religiously proper to see Him in settings with people that were considered unclean and untouchable. This has been a guiding principle as I reach out to others.

Legendary for his anger and toughness, a former NFL player—now an assistant coach in the league—felt he had done too many bad things on the field to ever be good enough to be a Christian. His wife came to our church and experienced a life-changing encounter with Jesus. She had worked previously in Hollywood, running a public relations firm and as an author and a writer for television shows. She often mocked Christians because of their odd behavior. Her testimony now is, "I went from making fun of them to being one of them." Still, her husband kept his distance from any real dialogue about spiritual matters.

I began reaching out to him and could see that behind the toughness was a sensitivity and desire for God that was stunning. After a lot of prayer I invited him to join me on a trip to Israel. Amazingly, he agreed. From the time we landed, he was fully engaged. He kept saying things like, "This is real!"—meaning that the events and places mentioned in the Bible were actually true. After a few days of touring the city of Jerusalem, we went to the Galilee region, where Jesus spent a majority of His time and ministry. This man, who had been so tough on the outside, asked to be baptized in the Sea of Galilee. What seemed appropriate was the fact that we baptized him at the very place where Jesus cast out a legion of demons into the pigs. When he heard that story, he said, "This is the right place for me to be baptized." His wife and colleagues often remark at the difference Christ has made in this man's life, both on and off the field. This story is similar to millions of others, each one with pain and heartache that was overcome by the love of God.

Whether they are family members, classmates, or strangers you encounter through your job, there is the constant opportunity to show God's love in a practical way to others. Remember, there is no one too lost or too far away from God that His love cannot reach them. Or as Corrie Ten Boom, who suffered at the hands of the Nazis in a concentration camp and watched her beloved sister die from the abuse, would say, "There is no pit so deep, that God's love is not deeper still."

As we follow Jesus, we are committing not just to keeping a set of rules but following His example of love and compassion to the world around us. As you engage others with the gospel, and the reasons to believe, may this compassion and mercy fill your words and actions. As Jesus said, "Go and learn what this means: 'I desire compassion, and not sacrifice'" (Matthew 9:13 NASB).

APPROACH

In this process of evangelism, there is the inevitable moment when you approach someone with the gospel. This is what many people dread because of the potential awkwardness that has usually been associated with personal evangelism. The word *approach* as a noun is defined as, "a way of dealing with something; an act of speaking to someone for the first time about something, typically a proposal or request." As a verb, "come near or nearer to (someone or something) in distance; speak to (someone) for the first time about something, typically with a proposal or request." This word, *approach*, is an excellent description of the mind-set in evangelism that we need. The big question is, *how can we approach people with the gospel?*

We have all seen the awkward, abrupt, and rude methods. Most of us cringe when seeing this done by others, like the person on the airplane, witnessing to a fellow passenger in a loud voice that disturbs their fellow passengers. We need not only to be prepared to give reasons for the hope that is in us but also to do it with gentleness and respect. Whatever approach we use to engage others with the gospel must include that tone to our dialogue.

This was the prime motivation behind the second word I told you was important: *salt*. It stands for *start* a conversation; *ask* questions; *listen*; *tell* the story. This simple formula has helped literally thousands of people have the right approach to engaging others. We will explain this in greater detail in a moment, but you can see from Scripture and your own experiences how simple conversations can turn into significant encounters that lead to a presentation of the gospel.

Jesus Himself engaged in conversations with people in fairly normal circumstances that led to a deeper dialogue about His own identity and purpose. The opportunities to start conversations and ask questions of others are virtually endless. If you are willing to listen first to others before you try and share your story and perspective, you usually will find them listening more attentively.

A great evangelism process always includes teaching people to have a wise approach in starting the dialogue about the gospel. In needy areas where possibly a disaster or tragedy has taken place, it can come down to simply giving water, food, or comfort. Life is filled with opportunity to serve others. In fact, Jesus said, "The greatest among you will be your servant" (Matthew 23:11). Serving others involves meeting the deepest needs of their existence which is, at its root, exactly what Christ offers. Over the years I have seen many people with a variety of wise and winsome approaches to explaining the gospel to unbelievers.

The right approach usually involves understanding the context of the people to whom you are reaching out. This produces the empathy and understanding necessary to speak intelligently about someone's situation. When we go to various nations to share the love of Christ, it makes a huge difference to know the background of the people's faith or unbelief. Being effective in a nation like the Philippines requires a different approach than being on the campus at Berkeley in California.

Take for instance the Jewish people. I feel there is a deep sense of debt to them both spiritually and morally. The spiritual debt stems from the fact that virtually all the things we as Christians enjoy are rooted in the Jewish faith and are connected to the land of Israel. From the Old Testament prophets and writings, to the New Testament Gospels, the letters of Paul, and the Savior Jesus Christ, all of these writers and people were Jewish. There is an overwhelming sense of gratitude because of this fact.

There is also an enormous sense of moral debt that exists as well. For centuries, the Jewish people have been persecuted and expelled from country after country. Their chief persecutors have called themselves Christian, even though their actions betrayed commands and teaching of Jesus at their very core. The most unique command of Christ is to love our enemies. This would not inspire anyone to plan harm or retribution to anyone, much less the people that gave the Christians everything they hold dear. The message of Christ crucified and raised from the dead should be a liberating one, not an excuse to oppress or harm anyone.

When a Jewish person asks me about my Christianity and why I care about his people, those things I just mentioned are always on my mind. My confidence is that regardless of your country or ethnicity, the gospel should be the best news you've ever heard.

TOOLS

I have found that there are various things we call "tools" that can help people convey the gospel consistently and more effectively. They help you overcome the many types of obstacles in terms of people being willing to engage in a conversation. Movies such as *God's Not Dead* have been used to help start the conversation about spiritual things. Probably the most effective tool in history is *The Jesus Film*, seen by more than one billion people and translated into one hundred languages and dialects.

A simple tool that we developed that is being used in personal evangelism is "The God Test."[4] It consists of two sets of ten questions—one for those who say they believe in God and one for those who don't. The *salt* approach we mentioned is the basis for this conversation starter. It has been translated into many languages and is now available for free downloading at the App store on either Android or iPhone. It has thus far been downloaded in more than one hundred twenty countries.

Thousands of people of all ages have been trained to use the God Test and are testifying as to how this tool simplified the evangelism experience and made it actually something fun that they could look forward to. The questions you ask people from the God Test actually help you remember and easily retrieve the apologetic content that is applicable. Just reading a lot of books and listening to YouTube debates don't mean you will be effective in communicating the right message at the right time to someone who is a non-Christian. The God Test contains some of the key questions that people who don't believe in God must answer to make sense of our existence and our universal sense of right and wrong. If you follow the approach taught in *salt*, you will listen first to what people have to say about the questions you're asking and then patiently wait for the opportunity to speak. We have found that if you respect others by listening to them first, they will usually grant the same courtesy to you. We have had atheists actually thank us for a meaningful conversation without all the drama and tension that usually accompanies this kind of activity.

Frans Olivier in Cape Town has used the God Test to train at least ten thousand people in the last four years. Over four thousand have made decisions to follow Christ in South Africa. "Our mind-set toward evangelism was dramatically altered by the God Test. Evangelism is now a part of the normal Christian experience for most instead of the dreaded duty of a few."[5]

Peter Dusan, a campus pastor at Texas State University, has used the God Test as effectively as we've seen anywhere, training hundreds of students to share their faith with others consistently. In one week they conducted more than one thousand God Test conversations with students on campus. When he trains people to use this tool, he says, "If someone watches me share my faith with others, they tend to think that my effectiveness is due to my boldness and confidence as a person. If they see me using a tool like the God Test, they believe they can do it as well."[6]

Dr. Bill Bright, the founder of Campus Crusade developed the "Four Spiritual Laws," and tens of thousands of young people were given an effective tool to engage others with the gospel. Millions have come to Christ as a result. I could list other exceptional tools, from multimedia seminars to Christian rock bands, that have been instruments through which God's Spirit was able to utilize and get people's attention. Given the massive creativity that marks the age we live in, there are countless tools that can be developed to help start conversations that have eternal significance.

SUMMARY

The focus of this book has been to give you evidence that Jesus Christ is the true Son of God and the promised Messiah and

Savior of the world. Because this is true, then it is news that is meant to be shared with others. This is what evangelism is. A part of that is an area called apologetics, which means to give the reasons why this story is true. This is a charge of Scripture as well, to be prepared to give those reasons, but to do it with gentleness and respect. Our character is always on display when talking to people about Jesus Christ, not just the content of our message.

In this chapter we have offered a simple evangelism process that is represented by the word *great*. It stands for *gospel, reasons, empathy, approach,* and *tools*. These five steps can give you a clear road map forward to becoming an effective witness for Christ. When these principles are taught in a local congregations and the gift of the evangelist is functioning alongside other pastors and teachers, the result is an engaging church. This is a dynamic congregation that is literally impacting the world for the glory of Christ and His gospel.

EPILOGUE
BEYOND A
REASONABLE DOUBT

YOU SHOULD NOW HAVE A CLEAR GRASP OF THE evidence that Jesus lived and did the things the Gospels said He did and said the things the Gospels tell us He said. He is the promised Messiah, not a pagan myth. The real hope is that every person would be able to clearly communicate that evidence to others. Each of the chapters has been written to help you remember the key pieces of evidence that point to the fact that the Jesus of history is indeed the Christ of faith. In the end you must be able to engage someone else in a conversation that leads to a clear presentation of this gospel.

Because Jesus is the Messiah, the Son of God, and Savior of the world, then His message should be the preeminent focus of our lives. Regardless of your calling and occupation, the gospel should be your priority. The obstacles that stand in the way must be identified and removed. The fact that we face such resistance to make His focus our focus shows that there is an opposing, adversarial influence in the universe. To be committed to Christ means to have a mortal enemy that is dedicated to the task of stopping and discrediting your efforts.

More than thirty-five years ago, I was overwhelmed by fear, doubt, and unbelief. Religion was no match against those forces that dominated my life. I prayed, attended church, asked for God's help, and in the end felt a little silly because of my feeble, futile efforts. I completely understand why people who go through seasons of intense spiritual searching end up frustrated and disillusioned. Looking back in history, you can see similar experiences in the lives of people such as Augustine of Hippo (known as Saint Augustine) and John Wesley, the founder of the Methodist church, just to name a couple.

Augustine lived in the fifth century and was raised by a Christian mother. Her influence seemed no match for the seductive power of Manichee's philosophy that gave license to indulge in sexual immorality. In his *Confessions*, Augustine would chronicle his journey out of the darkness of unbelief due to the enormous grip that his sins had on his soul. He spoke of the enemies of the Christian faith dismissing the Scriptures with mockery and skepticism, reminiscent of the same struggle that happens in our day. Yet he would see through the emptiness of their answers and, even more, their lives. Because of the shallowness of those who opposed the gospel, Augustine decided to sincerely listen to those who could give an explanation of the difficulties he encountered when examining the Scriptures. He would write in his *Confessions*, "More and more my conviction grew that all the knotty problems and clever calumnies which those deceivers of ours had devised against the divine books could be dissolved."[1]

An awareness of the history of past events that he had accepted and to which he had given credibility gave Augustine the needed objectivity to be open to the truth of the events spoken of in the Scriptures.

> Then little by little, Lord, with a most gentle and merciful hand you touched and calmed my heart. I considered the innumerable things I believed which I had not seen, events which occurred when I was not present, such as many incidents in the history of the nations, many facts concerning places and cities which I had never seen, many things accepted on the word of friends, many from physicians, many from other people. Unless we believed what we were told, we would do nothing at all in this life.[2]

After seeing the emptiness and the contradictions in the writings of the philosophers and cynics, and comparing them to the truth and purity of Scripture, he would write:

> You persuaded me that the defect lay not with those who believed your books, which you have established with such great authority among almost all nations, but with those who did not believe them. Nor were they to be listened to who might say to me, "How do you know that these books were provided for the human race by the Spirit of the one true and utterly truthful God?" That very thing was a matter in which belief was of the greatest importance.[3]

He would eventually come to a dramatic moment when he would see through the doubts and accusations to the truth of the Scriptures and the gospel story, which would open his heart and allow the Holy Spirit to change and transform him. Your faith is not just a matter of knowing the right set of facts about God but of taking the step of trust to receive the work of His Spirit in your life.

When I think of the struggle to find faith and press through the doubts in the mind and the lusts in the heart, I find encouragement by reading how Augustine was able to press through this deadly gauntlet and become one of the great leaders, thinkers, and champions in church history.

The other individual, John Wesley, lived in the eighteenth century and made an enormous impact on the world that is still being felt today. However, before this would happen, he would suffer deeply from doubt, fear, and a debilitating anxiety about his lack of faith. Wesley would attempt to defeat these suffocating foes by indulging in religious activities.

He traveled from England to America and gave himself tirelessly to the spreading of the gospel. Yet in all of his efforts, he would testify of remaining lost himself. He would write in his journal in the year 1737:

> I went to America, to convert the Indians; but oh! who shall convert me? who is he that will deliver me from this evil heart of mischief? I have a fair summer religion. I can talk well; nay, and believe myself, while no danger is near; but let death look me in the face, and my spirit is troubled. Nor can I say, To die is gain![4]

A few days later he would write:

> It is now two years and almost four months since I left my native country in order to teach the Georgian Indians the

nature of Christianity. But what have I learned myself in the meantime? Why (what I the least of all suspected), that I who went to America to convert others was never myself converted to God. I am not mad, though I thus speak; but I speak the words of truth and soberness; if haply some of those who still dream may awake and see that as I am, so are they.[5]

Wesley didn't suffer from factual doubts about whether the story about Jesus' death and resurrection were true or whether the Scriptures were true, but from more of an emotional or psychological doubt. There are many like this who seem to be stuck in terms of going beyond a mere intellectual knowledge of God and accessing the promises of God as one might actually eat a meal instead of standing outside of the restaurant and gazing at the menu on the front door.

His story points us to another dimension of what faith is all about. Faith begins with believing what the evidence about Christ and the Scriptures say is true; but it then goes a step further into actually experiencing what the promises of God offer. This includes salvation, a new birth, the indwelling power of the Spirit, and victory over the fear and doubt that plague the mind and vex the soul. It was this kind of faith that delivered me from the clutches of mental and spiritual darkness when I was a third-year university student.

In fact, it happened for me the way it happened for Wesley. He knew what the Bible said about the importance of having faith in God. "Without faith it is impossible to please Him [God], for he who comes to God must believe that He is, and that He is a rewarder of the those who diligently seek Him" (Hebrews 11:6 NKJV). The conundrum was how to have that kind of faith. It seemed to me that faith was something that some special people possessed, not me. My question was the same as Wesley's: *How can I stop the doubts from dominating my thoughts?*

You see, there is always the opportunity to doubt. As we discussed, Christianity is true beyond a reasonable doubt, not possible doubt. What I needed was not to dwell on the possible reasons that my fears and doubts might be true but focus instead on the reasonableness of the Christian story and then act on the promises God was offering me. In fact, most of these promises are for "whoever." "For God so loved the world that He gave His only begotten Son, that whoever believes in Him should not perish but have everlasting life" (John 3:16 NKJV).

Then there is the kind of faith that moves mountains. It, too, is available to "whoever." "And Jesus answered saying to them, 'Have faith in God. Truly I say to you, whoever says to this mountain, "Be taken up and cast into the sea," and does not doubt in his heart, but believes that what he says is going to happen, it will be granted him'" (Mark 11:22–23 NASB). The book of Romans gives us directions into this kind of faith:

> For "everyone who calls on the name of the Lord will be saved."
>
> How then will they call on him in whom they have not believed? And how are they to believe in him of whom they have never heard? And how are they to hear without someone preaching? And how are they to preach unless they are sent? As it is written, "How beautiful are the feet of those who preach the good news!" But they have not all obeyed the gospel. For Isaiah says, "Lord, who has believed what he has heard from us?" So faith comes from hearing, and hearing through the word of Christ. (Romans 10:13–17 ESV)

While restating the opportunity for whoever, it goes on to say that faith comes by hearing the word of Christ. The secret is found in what you hear and hear repeatedly. If you continually listen to atheistic and skeptical rants against the faith, you will find yourself languishing in unbelief yourself. Don't get me wrong. I have spent countless hours reading and listening to the objections to the faith. However, there comes a time when you have pretty much heard the criticisms and you have to make a decision about to whom you are going to listen. In fact, writing this book brought me into the writings of many skeptics that were brazen and shameless in their relentless efforts to discredit the gospel and dissuade as many as possible from believing. In the end it only strengthened my resolve to get the message out to as many as possible that Jesus is the promised Savior and Messiah of the world. This happens through people hearing the gospel. As the Scripture said, "faith comes from hearing."

The more people hear the gospel, the better the chances they will believe. It's that simple. In the same way, the more I hear the gospel, the more my faith is strengthened. It's an amazing phenomenon: I sense my faith getting stronger the more I share it with others. That is why evangelism, or sharing the gospel with others, will do as much for you as it does for those who hear it.

This was the insight that John Wesley himself learned from his mentor, Peter Bohler, almost three hundred years ago. While continuing to be harassed by doubts, he approached Bohler and asked him the secret of finding real faith and thus real peace. It had become so troubling that Wesley considered ending his ministry of trying to help others if he was overcome by his own doubts. He recorded the dialogue with his mentor in his journal: "Immediately it struck into my mind, 'Leave off preaching.

How can you preach to others, who have not faith yourself?' I asked Bohler whether he thought I should leave it off or not. He answered, 'By no means.' I asked, 'But what can I preach?' He said, 'Preach faith till you have it; and then, because you have it, you will preach faith.'"[6]

He was told to preach faith until he got it. This meant spending time reciting the promises of God and what the Scripture says about constantly giving voice to fear and doubt. If faith can come to others because they hear your words, why can't you encourage yourself as you speak these life-giving words? That was exactly what Wesley began to do. The result was a dramatic impact on the world through the forming of thousands of congregations that now make up the Methodist church. As Bohler predicted, because Wesley found faith through preaching it, he went on to preach it with greater force and conviction.

May God grant us a multitude of men and women who will go beyond the academic study of Jesus Christ and give themselves totally to communicating His Word to a desperate and needy world. There is no greater cause, and there is no better time than now.

ACKNOWLEDGMENTS

I WANT TO THANK MY WIFE, JODY; AND MY CHILDREN, Charlie, Wyatt, William, Louisa, and Elizabeth; for all their support during the months it took to research and write this book. I'm grateful to pastors James and Debbie Lowe and the Bethel World Outreach Church family for their prayers and encouragement. They are truly dedicated to reaching out to the people in the greater Nashville area and beyond with the message of the gospel of Jesus Christ.

It is a privilege to work with Dr. Brian Miller, who not only helped with the research in this book and in giving helpful input but also travels the world, speaking to thousands of students and professors about the evidence for God and the truth of the Christian faith. I'm grateful for my friends Dr. Gary Habermas, Dr. Craig Keener, Dr. Sean McDowell, Dr. Stephen Meyer, and Jim Wallace, who read the manuscript and gave input. It is an honor to have such a dream team of academic advisers.

The same should be said for the Every Nation Ministries leaders with whom I have worked for more than thirty years. Thank you, Ron and Lynette Lewis, Steve and Deborah Murrell, Brett and Cynthia Fuller, Kevin and Renee York, Jim and Cathy Laffoon, Phil and Karen Bonasso, Ferdie and Judy Cabiling, Frans and Deb Olivier, Tim and Lychelle Johnson, Russ and Debbie Austin, Bert and Shelia Thomson, Joey and Marie Bonafacio, Dave and Amy Polus, Mike and Julie Gowans, Lance and Dee Phillips, Brock and Allison Lillis, Brian and Chavonne Taylor, J. T. and Shelly McCraw, and the entire ministry team dedicated to reaching every nation in our generation.

There are so many others to thank that have made a difference in our lives. Troy and Tracy Duhon, Kelly and Joni Womack, Dale and Joan Evrist, Bob and Candy Major, Greg and Marlene Chapman, Sol and Wini Arledge, Steve and Cindy Hollander, and Danny and Diane McDaniel. I also want to thank Matt Baugher, Paula Major, and Lori Cloud from W Publishing Group at Thomas Nelson for their faith in this project and their continued efforts to spread the message of this book.

It has been an honor to work with Michael Scott, David A. R. White, and the late Russell Wolfe from PureFlix Entertainment in the movie series *God's Not Dead*. Thanks also to the screenwriters, Chuck Konzleman and Cary Solomon; and the directors, Harold Kronk and Brittany Lefebvre. I look forward to future projects in this series.

I want to thank the young people involved in the ministry of Every Nation Campus. Every day thousands of students are being engaged with the gospel through the efforts of the leaders as well as the students themselves. Together we are working toward the goal of reaching every nation and every campus.

Notes

Introduction: It Is a Thing Most Wonderful

1. "America's Changing Religious Landscape," Pew Research Center, May 12, 2015, www.pewforum.org/2015/05/12/americas-changing-religious-landscape/.

2. Richard Dawkins and Rowan Williams, Archbishop of Canterbury, "Nature of human beings and the question of their ultimate origin," discussion at University of Oxford, February 23, 2012, YouTube video, 11:00, posted by "Anglican08," February 24, 2012, https://www.youtube.com/watch?v=HfQk4NfW7g0.

3. "It Is a Thing Most Wonderful," words by William Walsham How (1823–1897), 1872.

4. "We've a Story to Tell to the Nations," words by H. Ernest Nichol (1862–1928), 1896.

Chapter 1: Man, Myth, or Messiah?

1. Albert Schweitzer; W. Montgomery (trans.), *The Quest of the Historical Jesus*, (Minneapolis: Fortress Press, 2001; orig. 1910), 6.

2. SNL Transcripts, http://snltranscripts.jt.org/86/86qheaven.phtml.

3. Blaise Pascal, *Pascal's Pensées* (Radford, VA: Wilder Publications, 2011), 61.

4. Michael Shermer, "God's Number Is Up," *Scientific American*, July 2004, http://www.michaelshermer.com/2004/07/gods-number-is-up/.

5. Lawrence Krauss, Krauss discusses his book *A Universe from Nothing*, The Colbert Report, June 21, 2012, Comedy Central video, 5:00, http://www.cc.com/video-clips/e6ik9l/the-colbert-report-lawrence-krauss.

6. Stephen Hawking and Leonard Mlodinow, *The Grand Design* (New York: Bantam, 2010), 5.

7. Charles Darwin, *The Descent of Man*, 2nd ed. (Rand McNally & Company, 1874), 133–4.

8. J. Ed Komoszewski, M. James Sawyer, Daniel B. Wallace, *Reinventing Jesus: How Contemporary Skeptics Miss the Real Jesus and Mislead Popular Culture* (Grand Rapids: Kregel, 2006), 16.

9. W. J. Prior, "The Socratic Problem" in ed. Hugh H. Benson, *A Companion to Plato* (West Sussex, UK: Blackwell, 2006), 25–35.

10. Reza Aslan, *Zealot: The Life and Times of Jesus of Nazareth* (New York: Random House, 2013), 35.

11. John Veitch, *The Meditations and Selections from the Principles, of René Descartes* (Sacramento: BiblioLife, 2009), 130.

12. Schweitzer, *The Quest of the Historical Jesus*, 478.

13. Craig S. Keener, *The Historical Jesus of the Gospels* (Grand Rapids: Eerdmans, 2012), 15–17.

14. Stephen T. Davis, *Risen Indeed: Making Sense of the Resurrection* (Grand Rapids: Eerdmans, 1993), 192.

15. Michael Grant, *Jesus: An Historian's Review of the Gospels* (New York: Simon & Schuster, 1995), 182.

16. Will Durant, *The Story of Civilization: Part III, Caesar and Christ* (New York: Simon & Schuster, 1944).

17. N. T. Wright, *The New Testament and the Victory of God*, vol. 2 (Minneapolis: Fortress Press, 1996), 110.

18. Saint Augustine, *Confessions of St. Augustine*, 1.1.

19. Richard J. Evans, *In Defense of History* (New York: W. W. Norton, 1999), 219.

20. Gerald O'Collins, *Easter Faith: Believing in the Risen Jesus* (Mahwah, NJ: Paulist Press, 2003), 34.

Chapter 2: The Minimal Facts

1. Michael Licona, in Lee Strobel, *The Case for the Real Jesus: A Journalist Investigates Current Attacks on the Identity of Christ* (Grand Rapids: Zondervan, 2007), 112.

2. Gary R. Habermas, "The Minimal Facts Approach to the Resurrection of Jesus: The Role of Methodology as a Crucial Component in Establishing Historicity," August 2, 2012, http://www.garyhabermas.com/articles/southeastern_theological_review/minimal-facts-methodology_08-02-2012.htm.

3. Michael R. Licona, *The Resurrection of Jesus: A New Historiographical Approach* (Downers Grove, IL: InterVarsity Press, 2010), 28.

4. Paul L. Maier, *In the Fullness of Time: A Historian Looks at Christmas, Easter, and the Early Church* (San Francisco: HarperCollins, 1991), 197.

5. Craig S. Keener, "Assumptions in Historical Jesus Research: Using Ancient Biographies and Disciples' Traditioning as a Control," *Journal for the Study of the Historical Jesus* 9 (2011), 30.

6. Richard Dawkins, "Has Science Buried God," 2008 Richard Dawkins v. John Lennox debate sponsored by Fixed Point Foundation, Dawkins admits Jesus existed, YouTube video, 0:39, posted by "fusion channel," April 12, 2014, https://www.youtube.com/watch?v=Ant5HS01tBQ.

7. Bart D. Ehrman, *Did Jesus Exist? The Historical Argument for Jesus of Nazareth* (New York: HarperOne, 2012), 7.

8. William Edward Hartpole Lecky, *History of European Morals, from Augustus to Charlemagne* (New York: D. Appleton, 1897), 2:8–9.

9. Flavius Josephus, *Antiquities of the Jews*, 18.63–64.

10. Tacitus, *Annals*, 15.44.

11. Lucian of Samosata, *The Works of Lucian of Samosata*, trans. H. W. Fowler (Digireads.com), 472.

12. Jacob Neusner, trans. *The Talmud of Babylonia: Sanhedrin* (Tampa: University of South Florida, 1984), 43A.

13. John T. Carroll and Joel B. Green, *Death of Jesus in Early Christianity* (Peabody, MA: Hendrickson, 1995), 166. See also page 21, where Jesus' death is considered a "virtual certainty."

14. Gary R. Habermas and Michael Licona, *The Case for the Resurrection of Jesus* (Grand Rapids: Kregel, 2004), 70.

15. Habermas, "The Minimal Facts Approach to the Resurrection of Jesus."

16. N. T. Wright, *The Resurrection of the Son of God* (Minneapolis: Fortress Press, 2003), 3:686–96.

17. *Digesta Iustiniani: Liber 48* (Mommsen and Krueger), 48.24.3, accessed April 13, 2014, http://droitromain.upmf-grenoble.fr /Corpus/d-48.htm.

18. Flavius Josephus, *The Works of Josephus: Complete and Unabridged*, trans. William Whiston, new upd. ed. (Peabody, MA: Hendrickson, 1987), 798.

19. Craig A. Evans, "Getting the Burial Traditions and Evidence Right," in *How God Became Jesus: The Real Origins of Belief in Jesus' Divine Nature—A Response to Bart D. Ehrman*, ed. Michael F. Bird (Grand Rapids: Zondervan, 2014), 76; also see pages 71–93.

20. Craig Keener, personal correspondence to author, August 19, 2015.

21. Luke Timothy Johnson, *The Writings of the New Testament: An Interpretation* (Philadelphia: Fortress Press, 1986), 96–97 (emphasis in original).

22. Josephus, *Antiquities of the Jews*, 20.9.1.

23. Sean McDowell, "Did the Apostles Really Die as Martyrs for Their Faith?" *Biola* magazine, Fall 2013, http://magazine.biola .edu/article/13-fall/did-the-apostles-really-die-as-martyrs-for -their-f/.

24. Craig S. Keener, *Acts: An Exegetical Commentary* (Grand Rapids: Baker, 2012), 1:271–304.

25. Gary R. Habermas, *Evidence for the Historical Jesus: Is the Jesus of History the Christ of Faith?* e-book, rev. ed. (June 2015), 16; www .garyhabermas.com/evidence.

26. "Evidence for the Resurrection: Minimal Facts Approach," *Ratio Christi—Campus Apologetics Alliance*, http://ratiochristi.org/uah /blog/post/evidence-for-the-resurrection-minimal-facts-approach.

27. Eusebius, *Church History*, 2.25.8.

28. Habermas and Licona, *The Case for the Resurrection of Jesus*, 65.

29. Josephus, *Antiquities of the Jews*, 20.200.

30. Robert L. Web, "Jesus' Baptism: Its Historicity and Implications," Bible.org, August 2, 2005, https://bible.org/article/jesus-baptism -its-historicity-and-implications.

31. For example, E. P. Sanders, *Jesus and Judaism* (Philadelphia: Fortress, 1985), 11.

Chapter 3: We Can Trust the Gospels

1. F. F. Bruce, *The New Testament Documents—Are They Reliable?* (Grand Rapids: Eerdmans, 1981), 90–91.

2. Michael R. Licona, *The Resurrection of Jesus: A New Historiographical Approach* (Downers Grove, IL: InterVarsity Press, 2010), 176.

3. Reza Aslan, *Zealot: The Life and Times of Jesus of Nazareth* (New York: Random House, 2013), xxvi.

4. For additional information, see F. F. Bruce, *The Canon of Scripture* (Downers Grove, IL: InterVarsity Press, 1988); and Richard Bauckham, *Jesus and the Eyewitnesses* (Grand Rapids: Eerdmans, 2006). However, Bauckham does present a different view on the authorship of John.

5. Irenaeus, *Against Heresies*, 3.1.1.

6. Eusebius, *Church History*, 3.39.

7. Bauckham, *Jesus and the Eyewitnesses*, 155.

8. Eusebius, *Church History*, 3.39.

9. James Patrick Holding, *Trusting the New Testament* (Maitland, FL: Xulon Press, 2009), http://www.tektonics.org/ntdocdef/mattdef.php.

10. Irenaeus, *Against Heresies*, 3.1.1.

11. Ibid., 3.14.1.

12. Eusebius, *Church History*, 6.14.5–7.

13. Quintus Tertullian, *Against Marcion*, 4.5.

14. Eusebius, *Church History*, 6.25.6.

15. Irenaeus, *Against Heresies*, 3.1.1; 2.22.5; 3.3.4. See also Keith Thompson, "Who Wrote the Gospels?," Answering Islam: A Christian-Muslim Dialog, http://www.answering-islam.org /authors/thompson/gospel_authorship.htm.

16. Brent Nongbri, "The Use and Abuse of P52: Papyrological Pitfalls in the Dating of the Fourth Gospel," *Harvard Theological Review* 98, no. 1 (August 2, 2005): 23–48, http://journals.cambridge.org /action/displayAbstract?fromPage=online&aid=327943.

17. Daniel B. Wallace, "Daniel B. Wallace on the New Testament Documents," *Apologetics 315* (blog), July 8, 2012, http://www .apologetics315.com/2012/07/daniel-b-wallace-on-new -testament.html.

18. Jona Lendering, "Alexander the Great: the 'good' sources," Livius .org, http://www.livius.org/aj-al/alexander/alexander_z1b.html.

19. Robin Seager, *Tiberius* (Malden, MA: Wiley-Blackwell, 2005), 232–42. The one commonly cited very early source is Velleius Paterculus, who was a contemporary of Tiberius. However, a general concern for his writings is extreme bias.

20. John W. Wenham, *Christ and the Bible* (Grand Rapids: Baker, 1984), 187; Craig Bloomberg, *Can We Still Believe the Bible?: An Evangelical Engagement with Contemporary Questions* (Grand Rapids: Brazos Press, 2014), 27.

21. Craig S. Keener, *Acts: An Exegetical Commentary* (Grand Rapids: Baker, 2013), 3:289–94.

22. Mark D. Roberts, *Can We Trust the Gospels?: Investigating the Reliability of Matthew, Mark, Luke, and John* (Wheaton, IL: Crossway, 2007), 64.

23. Ibid., 157.

24. Ibid., 133.

25. Keener, *Acts*, 2:216.

26. Robin Schumacher, "The Gospel According to Bart Ehrman," *Apologetics 315* (blog), July 8, 2013, http://www.apologetics315.com/2013/07/the-gospel-according-to-bart-ehrman.html.

27. Mark Shea, "Discrepancies in the Gospels," © 2007, Mark-Shea.com, http://www.mark-shea.com/ditg.html.

28. J. Warner Wallace, *Cold Case Christianity* (Colorado Springs: David C. Cook, 2013).

29. Craig Blomberg, *Historical Reliability of the Gospels* (Downers Grove, IL: InterVarsity Press, 1987), 203–4.

30. Ibid., 248.

Chapter 4: The Crucifixion

1. The Greek word used in the Gospels for *hand* also includes the wrist and forearm.

2. The full medical and historical details of Jesus' death are described in the following article: William D. Edwards, Wesley J. Gabel, and Floyd E. Hosmer, "On the Physical Death of Jesus Christ," *JAMA* 255, no. 11 (March 21, 1986): 1455–63.

3. Ann Gauger and Douglas Axe, *Science of Human Origins* (Seattle: Discovery Institute Press, 2012), 45–84.

4. Ibid., 105–22.

5. For a detailed argument, see C. S. Lewis, *Mere Christianity*.

6. For a detailed treatment of this topic, see Brian Dodd, *The Problem with Paul* (Downers Grove, IL: InterVarsity Press, 1996); or Craig S. Keener and Glenn Usry's *Defending Black Faith: Answers to Tough Questions About African-American Christianity* (Downers Grove, IL: InterVarsity Press, 1997).

Chapter 5: The Resurrection

1. Gary R. Habermas, "My Pilgrimage from Atheism to Theism: An Exclusive Interview with Former British Atheist Professor Antony Flew." Available at http://www.deism.com/antony_flew_Deism_interview.pdf.

2. Karl Popper, *The Logic of Scientific Discovery* (New York: Routledge, 1959).

3. William Lane Craig and Sean McDowell, "Should Christians apologize for their faith?," Fervr, February 24, 2013, http://fervr .net/bible/should-christians-apologize-for-their-faith.

4. N. T. Wright, *The Resurrection of the Son of God: Christian Origins and the Question of God* (Minneapolis: Fortress Press, 2003), 3:6.

5. Wolfhart Pannenberg, *Jesus—God and Man* (Philadelphia: Westminster Press, 1977), 109.

6. Joseph W. Bergeron and Gary R. Habermas, "The Resurrection of Jesus: A Clinical Review of Psychiatric Hypotheses for the Biblical Story of Easter," *Irish Theological Quarterly* 80, no. 2 (2015): 171; also see 157–72.

7. Matt Slick, "Jesus only appeared to have died on the cross— Swoon theory," CARM, https://carm.org/swoon-theory.

8. Lee Strobel, *The Case for Easter: A Journalist Investigates the Evidence for the Resurrection*, Kindle ed. (Grand Rapids: Zondervan, 2009), Kindle locations 279–,).

9. Bart Ehrman, *How Jesus Became God* (New York: HarperCollins, 2014), 164.

10. Dr. George Wood, personal interview with author, June 20, 2015, Juneau, Alaska.

11. Clement, *Letter to the Corinthians* 42.1–4.

12. Gary R. Habermas, "Video Debates and Lectures with Dr. Gary R. Habermas," http://garyhabermas.com/video/video.htm.

Chapter 6: Dispelling the Myths

1. J. Ed Komoszewski, M. James Sawyer, Daniel B. Wallace, *Reinventing Jesus: How Contemporary Skeptics Miss the Real Jesus and Mislead Popular Culture* (Grand Rapids: Kregel, 2006), 237.

2. For a fuller critique see James Patrick Holding, "Horus and Osiris vs Jesus," Tekton Apologetics, tektonics.org/copycat/osy.php.

3. Stephen J. Bedard, "Exposing the Spirit of the Age: A Response to the Zeitgeist Movie," *The Poached Egg*, April 9, 2013, www

.thepoachedegg.net/the-poached-egg/2013/04/exposing-the
-spirit-of-the-age-a-response-to-the-zeitgeist-movie.html.

4. Bart D. Ehrman, *Did Jesus Exist?: The Historical Argument for Jesus of Nazareth* (New York: HarperOne, 2012), 5.

5. Komoszewski, *Reinventing Jesus*, 234.

6. Ibid, 318.

7. Jonathan Z. Smith, "Dying and Rising Gods," *Encyclopedia of Religion*, 2nd ed. Lindsay Jones (Detroit: Macmillan, 2005 [original: 1987]), 4:2535. See also www.toughquestionsanswered .org/2012/10/08/what-are-the-parallels-between-jesus-and-the -divine-men-of-the-ancient-world-part-3/.

8. A classic example is Karen Armstrong, *History of God: The 4000-Year Quest of Judaism, Christianity and Islam* (New York: Random House, 1993).

9. James D. G. Dunn, *A New Perspective on Jesus: What the Quest for the Historical Jesus Missed* (Acadia Studies in Bible and Theology) (Grand Rapids: Baker, 2005), 44.

10. Ibid., 50.

11. William Lane Craig, *Reasonable Faith: Christian Truth and Apologetics* (Wheaton, IL: Good News, 2008), 391.

12. Craig S. Keener, *The Historical Jesus of the Gospels* (Grand Rapids: Eerdmans, 2009), 333.

13. Ehrman, *Did Jesus Exist?*, 26.

14. Richard Carrier, *On the Historicity of Jesus: Why We Might Have Reason for Doubt* (Sheffield, UK: Sheffield Phoenix Press, 2014).

15. Adapted from Alan Anderson, "The Alleged Parallels Between Jesus and Pagan Gods," *Examiner.com*, July 29, 2012, http://www .examiner.com/article/the-alleged-parallels-between-jesus-and -pagan-gods.

16. Michael J. Wilkins, *Jesus Under Fire: Modern Scholarship Reinvents the Historical Jesus* (Grand Rapids: Zondervan, 1995), 138.

17. Fitzedward Hall, trans. *Vishnu Purán: A System of Hindu Mythology and Tradition* (Amazon: Ulan Press, 2012), 4:294, https://archive.org.

18. Prayson Daniel, "Refuting Krishna Myth Parallelism to Christianity," *With All I Am*, April 26, 2011, https://withalliamgod.wordpress.com/2011/04/26/refuting-krishna-myth-parallelism-to-christianity/.
19. William Joseph Wilkins, *Hindu Mythology, Vedic and Puranic* (Boston: Elibron, 2005), 217–18.
20. Benjamin Walker, *The Hindu World: An Encyclopedic Survey of Hinduism* (New York: Praeger, 1983), 1:240–41.
21. Jack Finegan, *Myth and Mystery: An Introduction to the Pagan Religions of the Biblical World* (Grand Rapids: Baker, 1989), 203–7.
22. Ronald Nash, *The Gospel and the Greeks: Did the New Testament Borrow from Pagan Thought?* (Phillipsburg, NJ: P&R, 2003), 137.
23. Gary Lease, "Mithraism and Christianity: Borrowings and Transformations," in Wolfgan Haase, ed., *Aufsteig und Niedergang der Romischen Welt* (Germany: Walter de Gruyter, 1972), 2:1316.
24. Komoszewski, *Reinventing Jesus*, 226.
25. Ronald Nash, "Was the New Testament Influenced by Pagan Religions?," *Christian Research Journal* (Winter 1994): 8.
26. Ehrman, *Did Jesus Exist?*, 25.
27. The early Christians never claimed that Jesus was born on December 25.
28. For fuller treatment of responses to such pagan parallels, see Gregory A. Boyd, *The Jesus Legend: A Case for the Historical Reliability of the Synoptic Jesus Tradition* (Grand Rapids: Baker, 2007).

Chapter 7: Jesus the Messiah

1. Dr. Stephen Meyer, telephone interview with author, June 15, 2015.
2. Richard Dawkins, *River Out of Eden: A Darwinian View of Life* (London: Orion, 2004), 133.
3. Sam Harris, *Free Will* (New York: Simon & Schuster, 2012), 5.
4. Marvin Olasky and John Perry, *Monkey Business: The True Story of the Scopes Trial* (Nashville: Broadman, 2005), 160; http://historicalthinkingmatters.org/scopestrial/1/sources/48/fulltext/.

5. Craig S. Keener, *The Historical Jesus of the Gospels* (Grand Rapids: Eerdmans, 2012), 257.

6. William Lane Craig, *On Guard: Defending Your Faith with Reason and Precision* (Colorado Springs: David C. Cook, 2010), 199.

7. John Weldon, John Ankerberg, and Walter G. Kaiser, *The Case for Jesus the Messiah* (Bellingham, WA: ATRI, 2011), 223.

8. For a more extensive discussion, see "Dr. Michael Brown Reveals the Real Messiah," AskDrBrown.org, http://realmessiah.askdrbrown.org.

9. Michael L. Brown, *Answering Jewish Objections to Jesus: General and Historical Objections* (Grand Rapids: Baker, 2000), 3:49–85.

10. Charles Spurgeon, "God with Us," Metropolitan Tabernacle, December 26, 1875, Spurgeon Gems, http://www.spurgeongems.org/vols19-21/chs1270.pdf.

11. The exact calculation for the appearance of the Messiah is debated, but the fact that the expected time falls in the general time period of Jesus' ministry is generally agreed.

12. Craig, *On Guard*, 195.

13. For more in-depth discussion, see Richard Bauckham, *God Crucified: Monotheism and Christology in the New Testament* (Grand Rapids: Eerdmans, 1999); and Larry W. Hurtado, *Lord Jesus Christ: Devotion to Jesus in Earliest Christianity* (Grand Rapids: Eerdmans, 2000).

14. Borrowed perhaps from "He Is," words and music by Jeoffrey Benward and Jeff Silvey. © 1994 Birdwing Music, ASCAP/Shepherd's Fold Music (BMI). All rights reserved.

15. David Limbaugh, *The Emmaus Code: Finding Jesus in the Old Testament* (Regnery Publishing, 2015); Kindle version: Location 380–383).

Chapter 8: Miracles

1. Hwa Yung, in Craig S. Keener, *Miracles: The Credibility of the New Testament* (Grand Rapids: Baker, 2011), 264.

2. Craig S. Keener, *Miracles: The Credibility of the New Testament* (Grand Rapids: Baker, 2011), 264.

3. Rice Broocks, *God's Not Dead* (Nashville: W Publishing, 2013), chaps. 4 and 5.

4. John Lennox, *Miracles: Is Belief in the Supernatural Irrational?* (Amazon Digital Services, 2013), Kindle location 354–57.

5. Bart D. Ehrman, *Jesus: Apocalyptic Prophet of the New Millennium* (Oxford: Oxford University Press, 1999), 197–200.

6. Gerd Theissen and Annette Merz, *Historical Jesus: A Comprehensive Guide* (Minneapolis: Augsburg Fortress, 1996), 290.

7. Josephus, *Antiquities of the Jews*, 18.63–64.

8. Marcus Borg, *Jesus, A New Vision: Spirit, Culture, and the Life of Discipleship* (San Francisco: HarperCollins, 1987), 61.

9. Irenaeus, *Against Heresies*, 2.31.2–4.

10. Athanasius, *Letters* (AD 354), 49.9.

11. William Lane Craig, "The Problem of Miracles: A Historical and Philosophical Perspective," www.reasonablefaith.org/the-problem -of-miracles-a-historical-and-philosophical-perspective.

12. Keener, *Miracles*, 155.

13. C. G. Brown, "Study of the Therapeutic Effects of Proximal Intercessory Prayer (STEPP) on Auditory and Visual Impairments in Rural Mozambique," *Southern Medical Journal* 103, no. 9 (September 2010), http:// www.ncbi.nlm.nih.gov/pubmed/20686441. For descriptions of similar studies and responses to critics, see Candy Gunther Brow, *Testing Prayer: Science and Healing* (Cambridge, MA: Harvard University Press, 2012).

14. Blaise Pascal, *Pensées—Enhanced Version* (Grand Rapids: Christian Classics Ethereal Library, 2009), 128.

15. Keener, *Miracles*, 532.

16. Ibid., 570.

17. Richard Casdorph, *The Miracles: A Medical Doctor Says Yes to Miracles!* (New York: Logos International, 1976).

18. Summaries of the healings can be found at *Is There a God?*, "Ten Healing Miracles," http://is-there-a-god.info/life/tenhealings.shtml.

19. Gary R. Habermas, *The Risen Jesus & Future Hope* (Washington, DC: Rowman & Littlefield, 2003), 61.

Chapter 9: Following Jesus

1. Joey Bonifacio, *The LEGO Principle: The Power of Connecting to God and One Another* (Lake Mary, FL: Charisma House, 2012), 100.
2. "Daily News on Wars in the World and on New States," http://www.warsintheworld.com, accessed November 12, 2015.
3. Deborah Alcock, *Lessons on Early Church History* (London: Church of England Sunday School Institute, 1879), 56.
4. Bob Beltz, *Real Christianity* (Ventura, CA: Regal, 2006), 184–5.
5. Dietrich Bonhoeffer, *The Cost of Discipleship* (New York: SCM Press, 1959), 33.
6. Steve Murrell, *WikiChurch: Making Discipleship Engaging, Empowering, and Viral* (Lake Mary, FL: Charisma House, 2011), 90.
7. Ibid.
8. Charles Spurgeon, "Faith and Repentance Inseparable," Metropolitan Tabernacle, July 13, 1862, The Spurgeon Archive, http://www.spurgeon.org/sermons/0460.htm.
9. Rice Broocks and Steve Murrell, *The Purple Book: Biblical Foundations for Building Strong Disciples* (Grand Rapids: Zondervan, 2009), 10.
10. Murrell, *WikiChurch*, 130.
11. Dale Evrist, telephone interview with author, June 20, 2015.
12. Murrell, *WikiChurch*, 155–6.
13. Bonifacio, *The LEGO Principle*, 202.
14. Murrell, *WikiChurch*, 7.

Chapter 10: Defenders of the Faith

1. Bob Beltz, *Real Christianity* (Ventura, CA: Regal, 2006), 20.
2. Ferdie Cabiling, personal interview with author, August 10, 2015, Manila, Philippines.
3. Dr. Sean McDowell, personal interview with author, May 27, 2015, Apologetic Leadership Group gathering, Biola University, La Mirada, California.
4. For more information see "The God Test," http://www.thegodtest.org.

5. Frans Olivier, telephone interview with the author, June 14, 2015.

6. Peter Dusan, telephone interviews with the author, June 15 and October 12, 2015.

Epilogue: Beyond a Reasonable Doubt

1. Saint Augustine; Henry Chadwick, trans. *The Confessions* (Oxford: Oxford University Press, 1991), 93.

2. Ibid., 95.

3. Ibid., 96.

4. John Wesley, *The Journal of John Wesley* (Grand Rapids: Christian Classics Ethereal Library, 2009), Kindle Locations 757–61.

5. Ibid., Kindle Locations 812–19.

6. Ibid., Kindle Locations 938–43.

Index

ABOUT THE AUTHOR

RICE BROOCKS IS COFOUNDER OF THE EVERY NATION family of churches, which currently has churches and campus ministries in more than seventy nations. He is also the senior minister of Bethel World Outreach Church in Nashville, Tennessee, a multiethnic, multisite church.

Rice is a graduate of Mississippi State University and holds a master's degree from Reformed Theological Seminary, Jackson, Mississippi, as well as a doctorate in missiology from Fuller Theological Seminary, Pasadena, California.

The author of several books, including *God's Not Dead*, *The Purple Book: Biblical Foundations for Building Strong Disciples*, and *Every Nation in Our Generation*, Rice lives in Franklin, Tennessee, with his wife, Jody, and their five children.

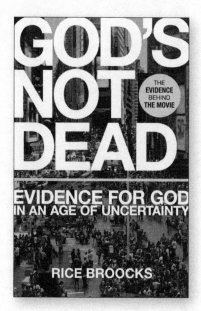

WHAT PEOPLE ARE SAYING ABOUT *GOD'S NOT DEAD*

"This is quite simply the most concise, punchiest, and wide-ranging argument for the existence of God and the truth of Christianity that has been written in recent years."

—DAVID AIKMAN, FORMER SENIOR
CORRESPONDENT, *TIME* MAGAZINE; AND
AUTHOR, *ONE NATION WITHOUT GOD?*

"*God's Not Dead* answers the thin case of the New Atheists, stirs Christians to confidence in their gospel, and empowers believers for both the spiritual and intellectual battles of our times."

—STEPHEN MANSFIELD, *NEW YORK
TIMES* BEST-SELLING AUTHOR

GOD'S NOT DEAD IS APOLOGETICS FOR THE TWENTY-FIRST CENTURY

Faith in God can be both intellectually satisfying and spiritually fulfilling. We are called to follow God and love Him with all our hearts *and* minds. This means we have to think and investigate.